Partnership in Secondary Initial Teacher Education

Edited by Anne Williams

David Fulto
Lo₁

David Fulton Publishers Ltd
2 Barbon Close, London WC1N 3JX

First published in Great Britain by
David Fulton Publishers 1995

British Library Cataloguing in Publication Data

A catalogue record for this book is available from the British Library

ISBN 1-85346-361-2

Typeset by Harrington & Co.
Printed in Great Britain by BPC Books and Journals, Exeter.

B/L 95   12.99

Contents

QUALITY IN SECONDARY SCHOOLS AND COLLEGES SERIES

Series Editor, Clyde Chitty

This new series publishes on a wide range of topics related to successful education for the 11–19 age group. It reflects the growing interest in whole-school curriculum planning, together with the effective teaching of individual subjects and themes. There will also be books devoted to management and administration, examinations and assessment, pastoral care strategies, relationships with parents and governors and the implications for school changes in teacher education.

Early titles include:

Active History in Key Stages 3 and 4
Alan Farmer and Peter Knight
1–85346–305–1

The Emerging 16–19 Curriculum: Policy and Provision
Jeremy Higham, Paul Sharp and David Yeomans
1–85346–389–2

English and Ability
Edited by Andrew Goodwyn
1–85346–299–3

English and the OFSTED Experience
Bob Bibby and Barrie Wade (with Trevor Dickinson)
1–85346–357–4

Geography 11–16: Rekindling Good Practice
Bill Marsden
1–85346–296–9

Heeding Heads: Secondary Heads and Educational Commentators in Dialogue
Edited by David Hustler, Tim Brighouse and Jean Rudduck
1–85346–358–2

Learning to Teach: a Guide for School-Based Initial and In-Service Training
Julian Stern
1–85346–371–X

The Literate Imagination: Renewing the Secondary English Curriculum
Bernard T. Harrison
1–85346–300–0

Managing the Learning of History
Richard Brown
1–85346–345–0

Moral Education and English
Ros McCulloch and Margaret Mathieson
1–85346–276–4

Series Editor's Foreword

This book has been written by a number of my colleagues in the School of Education at Birmingham University who are both involved with and extremely knowledgeable about initial teacher education at the secondary stage. It appears at a time when teacher educators throughout the country are busily implementing new programmes of work designed to meet the requirements of Department for Education (DfE) Circular 9/92. This envisaged a much greater role for schools and teachers in ITE – with schools being suitably reimbursed for their new responsibilities. Indeed, it soon became possible for schools wishing to do so to assume *total* responsibility for the professional preparation of teachers. And these 1993 school-centred pilot schemes received legislative approval in the 1994 Education Act which also removed the funding for teacher education institutions from the Higher Education Funding Council (HEFC) and handed it over to a Teacher Training Agency (TTA), a new quango with members appointed directly by the Education Secretary.

In Birmingham, many secondary schools have been keen to support the continued involvement of higher education in ITE – albeit at the price of receiving a comparatively low share of available resources. Both teachers and tutors are seen as having important and complementary roles to play in preparing students for a career in teaching; and there is welcome recognition of the fact that the students themselves can make a positive contribution to the life of the schools in which they are placed. The partnership model being developed is, in fact, one that can have distinct advantages for all concerned; and the point of this book is to describe and assess all the exciting forms it can take.

Clyde Chitty
Birmingham
March 1995

List of Contributors

All the contributors to this book work in the School of Education at the University of Birmingham where they are tutors to students on the PGCE course.

Graham Butt is a Lecturer in Geography Education. He is a member of the Geographical Association and has taught both PGCE and higher degree courses in geography education.

Carol Gray joined the PGCE team at Birmingham after twelve years of teaching Modern Foreign Languages in a variety of different schools. Her research interests are the use of IT as a Modern Foreign Languages resource and the delivery of Modern Foreign Languages to pupils with visual impairment.

Michael Grimmit is Director of the Centre for Religious Education Development and Research in the School of Education. He has published widely on all aspects of religious education.

John Hurman provides initial and in-service courses for teachers in the methodology and assessment of modern foreign languages, specialising in the teaching and examining of oral skills.

Susan Leach teaches the PGCE English course having been Head of English for many years in a Midlands comprehensive school. She is currently chair of Birmingham NATE and the author of several books on Shakespeare in the classroom.

Roger Lock is a Senior Lecturer in Science Education. His current research involves use of living organisms in science teaching and the public understanding of science with particular reference to the teaching of bioethics.

Pat Perks is currently a Lecturer in Mathematics Education. Prior to that she worked as an advisory teacher for nine years, working alongside teachers in primary and secondary classrooms. She taught mathematics in

Birmingham and was a head of department for nine years.

Stephanie Prestage taught mathematics in London and was head of department in a large mixed London comprehensive school. She is currently a Lecturer in Mathematics Education.

Heather Shilling is currently teaching the Postgraduate Certificate in Education Physical Education courses. She has previously taught on both B.Ed. and PGCE courses at Bedford College of Higher Education and Anstey College of Physical Education.

Allan Soares has taught in comprehensive schools in Bedfordshire and Staffordshire. He is currently involved in the initial teacher education programme for chemistry science students. His particular areas of interest include teacher assessment, equal opportunities in science and public understanding of science.

Maurice Tebbutt works mainly with those PGCE science students who have some specialism in physics but he also contributes to the courses provided for other science specialists. His main research interest for over ten years has been the use of computers in science education.

Ruth Watts is a Lecturer in Education (History), having taught history in secondary schools for many years. Her research and writing is on the history of education, women's history and the teaching of history.

Anne Williams is Senior Tutor for PGCE courses in the School of Education and a Senior Lecturer in Education (Physical Education). She has led the development of the partnership PGCE course at Birmingham.

Jeremy Woodhouse has worked as an advisory teacher for physical education and has taught both B.Ed. and PGCE courses. He is currently involved with the PGCE Physical Education course.

Preface

Since the publication of new requirements in 1992 for the training of secondary school teachers, universities, colleges and schools throughout England and Wales have faced the challenge of designing courses to meet changing demands. The expectation that schools will, in the future, be paid for their work with students, combined with a static or reducing level of funding has created severe tensions in some areas between higher education institutions and their local schools. Given all the other pressures under which schools currently work, it is perhaps surprising that most of these difficulties have been resolved and that a variety of partnership courses have been successfully launched, albeit with some reservations about their long-term sustainability. This book is about the approach taken by one higher education institution working with a large group of schools who wanted to retain a significant input to the course from university tutors and who chose to look for ways of working which would benefit pupils and teachers as well as the students for whom the course was designed.

Anne Williams
Birmingham
March 1995

CHAPTER 1

Setting the scene

This book looks at approaches to initial teacher education (ITE) partnerships which are based upon the principle that all partners – schools, pupils, teachers, tutors and students – can gain from the process of involvement with ITE through working in ways which are cost effective and which give benefits to all parties which will offset some of the costs incurred both by higher education and by the school.

A number of schools are concerned about the effect upon pupils of the need for student teachers to spend an increased amount of time there. Indeed a minority of schools have taken this to the point of marketing themselves as schools which, through opting out of any involvement with initial teacher education, can guarantee that their pupils will work only with qualified teachers. However, once the classroom is accepted as a place for students to be learning in other ways than simply by practising teaching whole classes, then the potential for many kinds of pupil benefit begins to emerge alongside clear benefits for the students involved.

A second important principle which has guided the writers' thinking in reshaping a postgraduate certificate course in partnership with teachers is that students are entitled to receive both broadly equitable treatment and also certain forms of experience which may be difficult to assure if students are placed across a large number of partner schools for the whole of their school-based work. For example, if students choose a university because of the opportunities offered to work in inner city schools, should they all be entitled to this experience? This is an issue for the course discussed here and was a consideration in discussing different partnership models.

The book is written as all of those involved with initial teacher education in the secondary phase, that is for 11–18 year olds, implement courses which have been revised to meet the requirements of Department for Education (DfE) Circular 9/92. This Circular represents the latest in a number of government initiatives which have provided a variety of new routes into teaching while exercising increased control over the content of training courses. It has been followed by an Education Bill which will remove control of ITE funding from the Council which funds the rest of higher education in England and which provides enabling legislation for schools who wish to train teachers independently of higher education.

Current proposals and emerging issues

The new requirements which have to be met by all courses of secondary ITE by September 1994, are based upon the principles that teachers should play a much larger part in ITE as leading partners and that schools should be reimbursed for the additional responsibilities which this will entail (DfE 1992). Schools wishing to take total responsibility for the professional preparation of teachers can already do so. School-centred pilot schemes were introduced in 1993, whereby funding, currently more generous than that given to partnership courses, goes direct to the lead school which may choose to involve higher education but which is under no requirement to do so. These schemes are legitimated in the longer term through Clause 12 in the Education Bill due to complete its passage through parliament during 1994. This states that:

> The governing body of any county, voluntary or maintained special school, or of any grant-maintained school, may provide courses of initial training for school teachers. (Education Bill 1994, clause 12)

Amid considerable debate about the real intentions behind the Bill and some scepticism about its overt purpose of increasing choice of provision among those who believe that the real purpose is to destroy the higher education component of ITE, many practical issues are also emerging. These include the way in which roles and responsibilities should be divided between schools and higher education institutions; how resources should be shared; and how, in an increasingly diverse system, students can be assured of a minimal level of equity in their treatment.

There is little agreement about the future role of the higher education institution. Lawlor continues to make no secret of her desire to see higher education's influence removed from the ITE process, commenting on Kenneth Clarke's proposals (Clarke 1992) with approval when she states that:

> young teachers will be sent to learn from senior teachers who have dedicated a lifetime to the art of imparting knowledge. (Lawlor 1992, p.16)

Her comment upon the moves towards more school-based courses which had already taken place leave no doubt about her conviction that student support should be the job of the teacher, not the HEI tutor.

Since classroom based training has been on the cards, university education departments have been busy devising more school-based courses. That is not the same as handing a young teacher over to a senior teacher. (ibid.)

Barber sees higher education as marginalised in terms of day to day involvement with student teachers although he defends the continued existence of departments of education for the purposes of admission of students, validation of courses, consultancy/INSET and research (Barber 1993). Berrill (1994) considers that higher education has forfeited the right to speak with any 'moral authority' on the ITE issue by arguing on the basis of self-interest rather than rationality. By opening a paper with the words 'In the future, when teacher education is based predominantly in schools...' (Berrill 1994) he gives a clear indication of the way in which he feels ITE should move. The relatively small numbers of school consortia currently bidding to run school-centred schemes suggests that his view is, at the time of writing, a minority one. The Secondary Heads Association advise any school contemplating 'going it alone' to proceed with caution (SHA 1993).

Other sources have seen the roles of schools and HEIs in the context of supporting students working in schools as being complementary. HMI, in a survey of school-based training (DES/HMI 1991), concluded that its success depends not only upon the quality of the relationship between the training institution and the school, and the level of the involvement of teachers in all aspects of the students' training, but also upon the active involvement of the tutor in supporting school-based work. They highlighted the quality of the support provided by classroom teachers as of particular significance, but also drew attention to the fact that the prime purpose of schools is to teach pupils, not to train students, and that not all teachers are either able or willing to take on a training role. The head of a school withdrawing from a partnership scheme endorses this view when he states:

While my colleagues and I have been trained to teach pupils, and believe we have considerable success in doing so, we do not claim to have all the skills or knowledge necessary to training students. Those of us who do have the potential and willingness to develop these skills are invariably in senior posts and heavily committed especially at a time of rapid change in schools. (Guardian, 17 May 1994, p.2)

Funding is high on the agenda as partnerships struggle to implement schemes which are demonstrably more expensive than their predecessors, witness the Articled Teacher Scheme (OHMCI 1993), within existing resource levels. In some parts of the country, notably Gloucestershire, schools have demanded a lion's share of the resources in return for providing most of the training. In others, including Nottingham, Birmingham and Sheffield, many schools have supported the continued involvement of higher education albeit at the price of a relatively low transfer of resources to them. Many schools appear to have little interest in playing a significantly increased role in ITE. Bolton, formerly HMI Chief Inspector, concludes that, 'To any prepared to listen it is clear that most schools do not want to assume the main responsibility for the training of teachers – even if the money were increased; they do not see it as their main task.' (Bolton 1994)

An important issue is that of what is expected in return for the money transferred. Barber (1993) points to the fact that there is too much focus upon the simple amount of money which is to be transferred to schools, rather than on what the money is actually for. The advice circulated by the Secondary Heads Association (SHA 1993), while acknowledging that there is no simple absolute answer to questions of how much money should be transferred, has suggested a global sum per student which, in SHA's view, schools should receive as a minimum. They have repeated the process for 1994. However there is no advice about what this money should be for, neither is there any recognition that students bring benefits as well as costs.

Wright (1993) offers a response to Barber's comment with an attempt to produce a formula which can be applied to the relative contributions of school and higher education institutions. He suggests that a needs based analysis of school costs or of HEI costs is of limited use when resources are so demonstrably inadequate to meet that need. His alternative is to examine the relative contributions of the partners and to divide the available resource in a proportion which reflects that. He suggests that first, relevant headings for expenditure need to be identified; second, such headings need to be given a weighting relative to their costs in relation to the total; and third, the respective school and university inputs need to be quantified in ratio or percentage terms. This would be one way of solving the problem of how to divide the resource equitably; however, HMI draw attention to the lack of accurate costing of the 'schools' contribution to training *relative to the benefits derived from students* (DES/HMI 1991, p.35, my emphasis).

This is a welcome comment upon the otherwise neglected benefit side of the equation and a recognition of the fact that students can contribute to the schools in which they are placed as well as taking from them. The neglect of school benefits may reflect the difficulty of actually costing the student contribution. It may also reflect the fact that there are many problems and 'grey areas'. For example, students do release staff time by teaching lessons, but the classes taught remain the responsibility of the class teacher and in subjects such as science and physical education, safety considerations limit the extent to which the class teacher can leave students completely alone. Staff development gains can be identified but are difficult to assess financially.

What is significant, is that these benefits do have a value which should be set against the real and perceived costs of working with students. This means that, whether or not it is possible to cost them with any real precision, they should be identified, articulated, and recognised during discussions about future course management and resourcing. Where alternative procedures are being considered, the benefits to the school, the teacher, the pupils and the students should all be considered, and, where the quality of the student experience is not compromised, strategies should be adopted which maximise the benefits to all involved.

There is also an issue about the most cost effective use of time and whether placing students in schools, singly or in pairs, for 24 weeks is the most appropriate structure, given that resources are so limited. The costs of subject-specific support will inevitably be very high. Some economies of scale are possible when dealing with whole-school issues, as demonstrated by institutions such as the Oxford Department of Educational Studies. However other partnerships, including our own, have been unable to get support for the minimum student numbers which such an arrangement requires. This was, in our case, at least partly through a desire to avoid setting up a system which discriminated against the involvement of small schools. It is also inevitable where numbers following different subjects vary significantly as is often the case. Determining policy here is related to issues about roles and responsibilities. If students are to receive teaching which is high quality as well as cost effective, there seems to be an argument for much more flexibility in school-based work and in student groupings over the course as a whole.

The Challenge

All of the activities described in this book have been offered within a partnership course in one institution. A decision of the schools, teachers and tutors, taken at an early stage in partnership discussions, was that the existing course structure should continue. That meant that students would be higher education based for 6 weeks during the early part of the Autumn Term and for a further 6 weeks at the beginning of the Summer Term. It also meant that the 24 weeks in school requirement would not be met by placing students singly or in pairs for the whole time, but would include the equivalent of up to 10 days where different subjects could propose their own patterns of work in schools. Thus, while Geography might choose to use 5 of these days for residential fieldwork, PE could choose to work in schools for two half days a week and Mathematics might decide to ask students to undertake a collaborative school-based project during the Summer Term. Figure 1.1 shows the course pattern through the year.

Figure 1.1

COURSE STRUCTURE AND
SCHOOL/UNIVERSITY DISTRIBUTION

School Experience			
2 week block	**PRIMARY SCHOOL**	PHASE 1	
	2 WEEKS		
	Roles/responsibilities negotiated by subject groups		
2 half days per week plus other time by negotiation	**UNIVERSITY/SCHOOL**	PHASE 2	*AUTUMN TERM*
	6 WEEKS		
	Roles/responsibilities negotiated		
3 week block	**SCHOOL**	PHASE 3	
	3 WEEKS		
1 week of preparation in school for the Spring Term block practice	**UNIVERSITY/SCHOOL**	PHASE 4	
	3 WEEKS		
	Roles/responsibilities negotiated		
13 week block	**SCHOOL**	PHASE 5	*SPRING TERM*
	13 WEEKS		
Time in school by negotiation plus field courses, e.g. in geography	Roles/responsibilities negotiated by subject groups **UNIVERSITY/SCHOOL**	PHASE 6	*SUMMER TERM*
	6 WEEKS		
3 week block	**PLACEMENT/DEBRIEF**	PHASE 7	
	3 WEEKS		

Several contributors consider approaches to partnership which involve working with large groups of students in one school to the potential benefit of all parties involved. Roger Lock and Allan Soares describe work undertaken with science students where tutors and partner school teachers organise whole day programmes for groups of students. Heather Shilling, Jeremy Woodhouse and Anne Williams discuss the different ways in which work with PE students early in the PGCE year can result in gains for teachers and pupils as well as for students. Michael Grimmitt examines a similar undertaking with RE students. Carol Gray and John Hurman look at intensive language days run in schools by Modern Languages students.

Others look at ways in which a whole cohort of students can have access to comparable experiences. Ruth Watts assesses work undertaken with History students which combines experience of site visit work for all students with contact with pupils from inner city multicultural schools. Maurice Tebbutt evaluates an exercise designed to develop all Physics students' capacity to use IT in their teaching in ways which benefit schools as well. Graham Butt describes a Geography field course planned and run by students for Year 10 pupils from a local school which aims to give all students an experience which will extend their understanding of fieldwork as well as their teaching skills while at the same time offering a course to school pupils which the school would find difficult to staff on its own.

In seeking to identify ways in which schools can benefit from working with students placed with them for major placements, Sue Leach discusses the experiences of a group of English mentors working in a partnership course for the first time. Finally there is an example of work which links the higher education based teaching with school-based work with the aim of both developing student understanding and skills and of sharing practice with schools in curriculum areas which are perceived as ones of possible weakness. Stephanie Prestage and Pat Perks describe how pupil assessment undertaken by students with mentors' help in schools is then moderated during a university-based session with tutors. The initiative for this came from the mentors who saw dissemination of practice from different schools, to be reported back to the schools by the students, as a benefit for both parties.

The approach taken

This book represents an action research approach to their work by a group of higher education tutors involved with the design and implementation of a revised course which has to meet statutory requirements in a way which makes optimum use of limited human resources and from which maximum benefit can accrue not only for the students, but also for the teachers, pupils and tutors involved. It is both a report of approaches to curriculum change in the context of ITE and a part of the action research process itself. The latter has occurred insofar as the exercise of meeting as a group to discuss one another's contributions has, at the same time, provided a forum for the evaluation of the early implementation of a range of new ideas together with an opportunity to consider alternative further developments. This has been important, not only for its immediate value to those involved, but also to satisfy what, for some (Hill and Kerber 1967), would be an important condition for successful action research, namely that the limitations of one individual trying to change his or her ideas and practice can be overcome through co-operative endeavour. Thus, what was already a co-operative endeavour undertaken by teachers, tutors and students working together, has gained from the insights brought by sharing with others involved in a similar process.

> Action research combines a substantive act with a research procedure; it is action disciplined by enquiry, a personal attempt at understanding while engaged with a process of improvement and reform. (Hopkins 1993, p.44)

This echoes Cohen and Manion's view that the prime feature of action research is that it is essentially an on-the-spot procedure designed to deal with a concrete problem located in an immediate situation (Cohen and Manion 1989, p.223). It is also often, although not always, characterised as practitioner led, as intended to solve a problem and as eclectic in its orientation. Cohen and Manion identify a further feature which is relevant to this book, namely that action research aims to bring about lasting benefit to the ongoing process itself rather than to some future occasion. This is especially relevant to the contributors to this book, all of whom have all been key players in the development and implementation of the work which they describe and all of whom are committed to its continuation and further refinement. They are all faced with the specific problem of implementing an ITE programme in partnership with teachers within severe resource constraints. Moreover, new programmes have to be developed in the context of what has gone before.

> Action research is appropriate…when a new approach is to be grafted onto an existing system. (Cohen and Manion 1989, p.226)

Because, in the tradition of action research, this book represents an account of work undertaken in response to a problem which, while impinging on ITE nationally, is being addressed in a specific context, its contents do not purport to be capable of generalisation to all ITE courses.

The specifics of the context include the past relationships with schools upon which the new course is being built; the locality – a large conurbation – of the higher education base; the extent of the changes required in order to satisfy the requirement of Circular 9/92 given that most students were already placed in schools for almost 24 weeks; the staffing situation within the higher education institution as well as that within particular schools; the financial unit of resource available to support ITE, which varies significantly from one institution to another; the nature of the course structure and management which encourages some diversity of practice between different subject groups but within a common framework. Nevertheless, we believe that, just as we have learnt from each other and gained ideas which we can adapt for our own use, so others working in ITE may be able to do the same. Some of what is presented here may be familiar to others working in the same subject area, but less so to those from other curriculum areas. Other elements represent departures from previous practice in response to a new situation. We hope that all are examples of action research undertaken with the aim of improving professional practice in the context of implementing innovation and change within an ongoing system (Cohen and Manion 1989, p.219)

While the writers are all based in the higher education institution, their reports are based upon evidence collected from many of those involved in the work carried out: pupils, teachers, senior school staff and the students themselves. This satisfies another requirement of action research, namely that those actually involved in the process should constitute a part of the data collected.

The context for this book is one of sustained attack on ITE, particularly on higher education, which until recently enjoyed a virtual monopoly of ITE provision. The common features of these attacks are that courses are ineffective, that they involve too little time spent in schools working with pupils, and that they contain too much irrelevant theory. Lawlor (1990) expressed the view that the current training system should be abolished on the grounds that higher education institutions simply peddle trendy educational theories. Although her evidence base is limited to information gathered from reading prospectuses and despite the fact that she has never visited a teacher training institution, her views have been listened to by successive ministers of state for education. Anthony O'Hear, a philosophy professor has also gone on record as recommending the abolition of initial teacher training courses (O'Hear 1988) notwithstanding his membership of CATE (Committee for the Accreditation of Teacher Education), the body responsible for the accreditation of teacher training courses between 1984 and 1994. From within higher education, Hargreaves and others have added their voices to those who would like to see control of ITE removed from higher education and located firmly within the context of the school (Hargreaves 1990, Beardon *et al.* 1992).

Changes, both in place and proposed, have been legitimated in the belief, among their proponents, that control, content and location of teacher training are all wrong. Content is perceived to be over-theoretical, although this would be strongly challenged by many initial training institutions, and there is certainly plenty of evidence of a shift away from theory, especially in postgraduate courses and particularly that which takes the form of the study of the disciplines of education. The location is perceived to have been biased heavily in favour of the training institution rather than the school which is viewed as the most appropriate location for the training of the prospective teacher. Control is seen to have been vested far too heavily in the training institutions, despite the influence of CATE, which had the power to withhold accreditation from courses which fail to meet its criteria for their approval.

In 1993, following a number of initiatives such as the Licensed and Articled Teacher Schemes which either increased the involvement of schools and teachers in the training process or gave them total control of it, and having increased significantly the involvement of schools and teachers in all ITE courses through Circular 9/92, John Patten, Secretary of State for Education, published a further paper on the reform of ITE (DfE 1993). This put forward proposals for the creation of a new funding agency for ITE, the Teacher Training Agency, and for legislation to enable schools to run initial training courses independently of higher education. It is perhaps not surprising that many in higher education and in schools challenge the government's assurances that all that is being promoted is quality and choice (see Patten in Hansard, 3 May 1994). As Edwards points out:

> Occasional ministerial assurances that the Government remained committed to the education department's continued and substantial role in teacher education have had to be placed in the context of a systematically hostile campaign from the political Right and of a sequence of reforms designed to promote more school-based, school-centred and school-provided training. (Edwards 1994, p.145)

Summary

Teacher education faces unprecedented challenges at the present time. The very pressures created by constant change within a very short timescale make it all the more important to stand back and assess what is being undertaken, both on a large scale and within specific elements of course provision. This book attempts to do just that in relation to specific aspects of provision with the aim of maintaining or improving the quality of ITE whoever the provider might be.

CHAPTER 2

Partnership in English: an investigation into the experiences of mentors as reflective practitioners

I want to start by suggesting that there are two crucial considerations that underlie the enterprise of educating student teachers, which remain central throughout a teacher's working life: first, the capacity to establish and maintain an inner conviction and commitment to the education of children and belief in their infinite capacity to learn, what we might call the idealism of teaching; second, an ability to reflect on what has been experienced and undertaken, in order to reshape and reorder existing practice and its underlying theory. Of course, these considerations are bound together: capacity to be idealistic presupposes some degree of reflection, and reflection implies some probing and weighing up prompted by perceptions of inadequacy, that is, of falling short of an ideal.

> Policy should be designed to cherish and restore the sense of idealism which is at the core of all good teaching, and to provide the opportunity for teachers to work constantly at refining and developing their skills. (Barber 1994 (*TES*, 18 March))

Barber's timely reminder of the importance of idealism as part of the irreducible mindset of teachers runs counter to many of the prevailing reductive, narrowing views of what teaching is, and therefore about what it is necessary to teach student teachers. But, as my survey confirms in several instances, it is this idealism, this reaching beyond the confines of the here and now, which teachers feel the need to preserve as part of their professionalism. Barber's article develops his theme to include more precise definitions, including: 'motivating pupils and maintaining high expectations while promoting pupils' self-esteem and a belief in the unlimited potential of pupils'. A recurring theme in official statements about the current state of education is the prevalence of low expectations held by teachers of their pupils. As an anecdotal illustration of this, a student teacher of English in the 1993–94 cohort reported being actively discouraged from attempting some ambitious work with a Year 8 class in a predominantly Asian school, because 'they won't be able to cope with it'. The student persevered, nevertheless, and successfully encouraged these pupils to complete this work and to gain a sense of achievement from it. Apart from raising questions of student/mentor relationship, this episode usefully illustrates the reactions of teachers to the unremitting daily pressure of grappling pedagogically with pupils whose motivations appear to lie elsewhere. For teachers inclined to react as this one did to the student's idea for a lesson, Barber's restatement of the place of idealism is fundamental. Teachers need, through a variety of means, to be helped to retain their own idealisms.

The second of my initial propositions, that is, the importance of reflection in the teacher's professional practice, formed the basis of my survey of English mentors: I was interested to find out, through interviewing teacher mentors, to what extent they felt that acting as mentors had encouraged them to reflect on their own practice. Reflection, and the exhortation to reflect, has become fundamental to what might be called the 'professional armoury' of teachers, and its development is an integral part of the recommendations for the training of student teachers. Hargreaves *et al.* recognised that the ability to reflect is not quickly acquired:

> This process of becoming a 'reflective practitioner' cannot be fully achieved in initial training, but is an inherent part of the professional development of all teachers after ITT'. (Beardon, Booth, Hargreaves and Reiss 1992, p.23)

while others recognise the very broad, generalised interpretations of the term:

> Trainees are today constantly urged to reflect, though it is not always made explicit what reflection means or what they should be reflecting on. (Maynard and Furlong 1993, p.76)

and identify an area of concern which continues to need addressing by collaboration between schools and the HE institution:

> Studies of practice have found that too often trainees' and co-operating teachers' reflections centre superficially on issues such as whether a particular strategy 'worked', on the children's apparent enjoyment of an activity or whether specified objectives had been met – in essence focusing on the 'safe' and not the 'challenging', on the 'existing' and not the 'possible'. (ibid., p.76)

This problem is made particularly acute where a mentor finds it difficult to move beyond the 'safe', and where the insecurities of the student teacher make these narrow certainties attractive. In working towards becoming a reflective practitioner, achieving the ability to reflect expressed as 'learning something wider and of more significance by making the tacit explicit', students and teachers are attempting to theorise, among other things, the 'constant, unremitting self confrontation' which characterises the process of teaching' (ibid.).

Whatever the difficulties and challenges posed by the practice of reflection, it is only through reflection, undertaken alongside, and as a result of, collaboration, discussion with colleagues, personal experience and observation, in-service training, and reading, that teachers can be enabled continually to inspect, refine, analyse and improve their own practice. The development of a conscious and continual process of trying to 'develop explanations about the pupils, the interactions in the classroom and about the processes of teaching and learning', as well as to 'examine the adequacy of theories about pedagogical contexts and processes and develop a critique of them' (Frost 1993, p.140) is crucial to the whole project of education.

Already extant, more precisely developed theories about the function of reflection are helpful in further consideration of the implications of the kind of investigation I have undertaken here. Griffiths and Tann (1992), for example, suggest five levels of reflection: reaction, repair, review, research, retheorising and reformulating, a continuum of response which elegantly defines the recursive nature of reflection, and provides a useful organising structure for 'reflecting' about 'reflection'. Opportunities to pursue reflective considerations of their own experience using such a structure would undoubtedly help mentors in developing their own practice further along the route they have already mapped out.

Discussion of the symbiosis between reflection and theory, and of the current trend for reflection, a personal kind of theorising, to replace 'theory' of the public, disciplinary kind, in educational discourse, could also usefully be undertaken as part of a continuing interrogation of the role of the schools *vis-à-vis* the role of the higher education institution in partnership. In our postmodern state, argues Wilkin, we are offered 'theoretical paralysis since theory has been dethroned and there are no transcendental qualities or experiences to which we can appeal. But it (post modernism) also offers an arena in which all voices will be heard with equal favour' (Wilkin 1993, p.46). It is in this spirit of being heard with 'equal favour' that the voices of the participating mentors are reported here, and in the spirit of the following that I offer commentaries on them:

It is no longer a question of relating disciplinary theory to practice (constantly advocated in the past but rarely demonstrated) but of relating one form of theory (personal theory) to any other form of publicly available theory which will perform the function of challenging the personal viewpoint. (Wilkin 1993, p.48)

There is one further consideration which I want to include at this point: because of the changes in LEA funding, and devolution to schools of the INSET budgets, the provision of subject specific LEA-provided INSET has diminished markedly. Bines observes that this devolution of funding has led to a focus on immediate, and institutionally-based, training requirements (Bines 1992), and Haigh describes the provision by schools of INSET intended to address issues of differentiation; the role of the form tutor; IT; pace and rigour; teaching and learning styles; in short, a wide range of cross-school, cross-curricular issues which may intersect with the main concerns of English teachers, but which are not primarily addressed to them (Haigh 1994). In this context, the response of teachers to the presence of students in school, and to the ongoing discussions and collaborations with the HE institution implicit in partnership, indicates the continued need for subject-specific INSET. Some of the replies given in this survey indicate how some teachers are able to capitalise on their mentor role to bring about their own professional development.

I set up the survey after PGCE students in English (1993–94) had completed their whole term placements in schools, when I invited some of the mentors with whom I had worked to talk through the central question: to what extent did the mentoring role encourage reflection about teachers' own practice? As I had been engaged in the process of observing student teachers in the classroom for the first time as a university tutor, I was continually struck by the tide of introspection which this induced: ranging from self-questioning of the most basic kind to considerations like: how do my own professionalism, my understanding of learning processes, my teaching 'craft' operate to allow me to judge whether a lesson has 'worked' or not? What educational as opposed to methodological considerations am I able to bring to bear on this lesson I am observing? What enables me to see that something which 'works' in the classroom, may also at the same time be educationally undesirable? Thoughts of this kind prompted me to ask: if observing lessons taught by students has this effect on me, what effect does it have on mentors who are engaged on a daily basis with students, their development, and their struggles?

The five mentors who participated represented between them a range of schools within the Birmingham area. It may be of some help to identify them according to the kind of school they work in:

Mentor A: Head of Department – inner city comprehensive, predominantly Asian pupils;

Mentor B: Head of Department – outer ring comprehensive, mainly white working class;

Mentor C: Head of Department – comprehensive in a nearby town, suburban, average middle class, white;

Mentor D: Second in Department outer ring comprehensive, mixed, mainly white;

Mentor E: Head of Department – Catholic comprehensive, mixed, predominantly white.

I focused the interviews round four sets of issues which I hoped would cover the main concerns of practising teachers, and which also took account of the CATE 9/92 student teacher competences, while allowing interviewees scope for further comments. The interviews were conducted informally, but quite tightly; discussion did depart from responding to the four initial questions I asked, if only to comment on some related aspect of mentoring, but always returned to the issue under discussion. My role was as a kind of participant interviewer, noting down what was said, prompting, pursuing lines of argument and probing where I felt teachers had more to say but had not yet found ways of articulating it.

Mentors were asked to talk about the following, in relation to the key questions: did the mentoring role encourage reflection about:
  – planning and preparation of lessons, including ideas, materials and approaches chosen?
  – classroom management, including discipline and organisation of the classroom as a learning environment?
  – teaching lessons, including relationships with pupils?
  – marking and assessment, and relating these to National Curriculum levels?

The most useful way to present mentors' detailed responses is to list their statements under the headings Positive and Negative, and to comment in turn on each set of responses. Statements have been identified by the letter name of each mentor.

Planning and preparation of lessons, including ideas, materials and approaches chosen

Positive

E Helping students prepare and think also helps the teacher to think through issues.

A Students' presence makes teachers think continually about what they are doing.

D Team-planning is exciting and thought-provoking.

D Working with students makes teachers think harder about what they want to achieve in lessons with pupils.

A Discussion on a daily basis helps the process of consideration and reflection.

D There is a long-term effect on the teaching of familiar lesson content from working with students.

E Students have a range of effects, including intellectual ones, making established teachers look afresh at expectations of what can be done with texts.

E Students affect approaches to literature generally.

D/A Students and their teaching had a direct effect on teachers' ideas about working on texts (examples given were: work on book covers before looking at text; work on newspapers; work on *Romeo and Juliet*).

B Students' skills and confidence with IT made the mentor realise that it was something she could also use in her teaching.

D Methodical planning of lessons with students improves the quality of mentor's lessons.

Negative

C Students had no effect because department used detailed schemes of work prepared prior to an OFSTED inspection.

B Students had no fundamental effect, even though the mentor did see that students are more adventurous.

B Mentor could see that students' expectations of pupils' abilities have some effect on teachers' views of what is possible.

Comment The statements here illustrate most importantly the ways in which mentors were prompted into thinking and reflection by experiencing regular, possibly daily, discussion with students. Their positive attitudes towards this, and recognition of the possibilities for change in their own practice which were opened up, seem to point to a general absence of such opportunities during the normal school year. For the four mentors who responded positively, this aspect of mentoring clearly stimulated much welcome thought, provided new ideas about ways of working with texts, and helped them tighten up their own planning and lesson quality. Significant words used by mentors were 'exciting', 'thought-provoking', 'look(ing) afresh', and seem to indicate how much teachers do need regular opportunities to rethink, and not necessarily those provided by external demands, such as the National Curriculum.

Where mentors appear not to have been prompted into positive reflection they may in fact have been tacitly indicating their own expertise by putting into practice 'the complexity and sophistication of experienced teachers' implicit planning' (McIntyre and Hagger 1993), that is, the highly developed skill of using schemes of work or other organising methods, as an explicit framework, while actually deciding on discrete lesson content and objectives without ever articulating them. For teachers who work like this, it may simply be much more difficult to see how the needs of students can influence their way of working. However, as McIntyre and Hagger point out in the same piece, in the context of collaborative teaching: 'the discipline of having to explain...one's purposes...and the (choice of) particular ways of pursuing these purposes can help mentors make explicit their own planning processes in a way that they would be most unlikely to do (otherwise)...' (McIntyre and Hagger 1993). Mentor D (third comment) appears not only to be making her purposes explicit, but finding opportunities to regenerate her own enthusiasm.

Classroom management, including discipline and organisation of the classroom as a learning environment

Positive

B Observation reaffirms teachers' views of what will and what will not work in the classroom, possibly leading to changes in their own practice.

B Watching another person teach is always a positive and useful experience.

C The observer (teacher) does not necessarily have the true measure of the student's lesson, which might succeed against the observer's expectations – an eye-opener, making teachers realise that they are not always necessarily right.

E As an observer it is much easier to ask the question: are children learning?

E Observing students' lessons makes teachers much more aware of the quiet, 'good', unnoticed pupils in the classroom.

E This awareness leads teachers to think about developing strategies for involving all the pupils in the lesson.

E Observation makes teachers realise how much teacher time is given to the attention-seekers in the class.

A Watching students make mistakes makes teachers wonder to what extent they do the same – for example, turning one's back to the class to write on the board.

Negative

D Little effect, although presence of students makes this mentor realise the danger of slipping into 'teacher pattern' – this comment also included under the heading of relationships with pupils.

Comment This group of very positive responses shows mentors' reactions in the observer role which they undertake whenever they watch students teach. It is significant that none of them comments on her thinking from within a team-teaching role, although some of them certainly worked like this with students. The significance of these comments lies in their perceptions of the classroom resulting from a changed focus. At the back of the room teachers see things that they perhaps do not notice from the front, such as the quiet, non-intrusive pupil and the ways in which attention seekers claim the teacher's time. The implication here is that teachers operate mostly from the front of the classroom, or that they rarely find (or make) opportunities to sit down with pupils in other parts of the room and to deflect the focal point of the lesson away from themselves. The observer role provides them with opportunities to evaluate themselves as well as the students, and also, particularly for mentors B and E, to see the need to set up new classroom procedures to cater for pupil needs which they have been newly alerted to.

These experienced teachers clearly find some of the revelations derived from sitting at the back of the room quite startling. Mentor C, for example, acknowledges that it was 'eye-opening' to realise that the teacher is not always right in his or her convictions of what will work and what will not work; this experience has been a significant learning one for her. The refocusing on pupils from this different vantage point, a realisation which underlies all the responses from Mentor E, confirms how teaching from the front of the room inevitably produces those invisible 'them and us' barriers which make it impossible for any teacher accurately to gauge whether children are learning or not. For all of them, observing students has in one way or another stimulated them to think about their own practice.

Teaching lessons, including relationships with pupils

Positive

D Helping students with differentiation and drafting gave one mentor a way of using strategies in a 'consciously sharp way', and helped prevent the sameness induced by familiarity.

D Students have difficulties in getting pupils to redraft, so there is also a learning process for the mentor in this area.

A Mentor made to think again about what she actually did in helping pupils redraft.

D Mentoring reminds teachers of the possibility of going beyond the obvious with texts and classroom work.

B Being observed, by students or other teachers, alters the way the teacher operates in the classroom; the teacher gives a 'good' lesson for the benefit of the observer.

B There is possibly a positive long-term effect on teachers' own teaching from being observed.

C Teachers' previous ideas of how to teach can be challenged by different methodology used by students.

C For a mentor who had a mature student on placement (a student with previous teaching experience) there was considerable INSET value in the mentoring role, and this teacher started using again methods which she had forgotten.

Relationships with pupils

E Students' presence prompted feelings of needing to regain freshness of interest in pupils, mentor admired students' ability to keep up very good one-to-one relationships with pupils.

E Teachers made to think about their own inclination to become cynical; makes teachers realise how hard it is to change out of the role of 'teacher'.

D Teachers are reminded of the need to be sensitive to pupils – student's method of approaching pupils reminded one mentor that confrontation was not the only way; she was reminded that more conciliatory methods do exist and that these are often preferable and extremely effective.

E Because teaching changes teachers, they lower their level of response to what pupils say, and fall into the habit of regarding it as inferior because the teacher is permanently cast in the role of being 'better'; mentor sees the need to keep an open mind, both to what pupils say and to what texts say, and to listen more.

E Incentive to listen to what individual pupils say disappears from teaching and relationships with pupils as teachers become more and more experienced; mentor feels strong desire to re-establish her ability to engage with pupils in this way.

C Watching student interact with pupils made her realise the extent to which she did not really listen to pupils – she would want to make greater efforts in that direction in future.

Negative

E Students had little influence on one mentor; her own flexibility and responsiveness to the dynamics of the classroom are what she is trying to pass on to the students.

Comment Comments from mentors A and D show an interesting focus on drafting and redrafting, suggesting that working with pupils individually on their writing is felt to be one of the key teaching interactions in the English classroom. It was obviously felt to be so in the context of working with students.

Other comments indicate again teachers' openness to other ideas and approaches, and the recognition (for mentor C) of the inadvertent INSET role performed by her mature student. Mentor B draws attention to the benefits for teachers of being observed themselves, indicating an unmet need for wider recognition from outside the classroom, and for different expectations to be exerted than those provided by pupils. The presence of students (or others) as observers seems to act as a stimulus, activating the teacher into more self-consciously alert teaching than usual.

The comments about relationships with pupils draw attention to the regret obviously felt by these three mentors that their years of experience have moved them further and further away from the 'freshness of interest' they once had in pupils and in what they had to say (elsewhere mentor C indicated how struck she had been by the student's genuine interest in everything pupils said), and the fact that they had in effect stopped listening to pupils. The annual presence of students acts as a welcome reminder to them of alternative ways of engaging with pupils, while also showing them how far they have fallen into 'teacher' role, and (for mentor D) how 'confrontation' rather than conciliation can so easily become a permanent mode of interaction.

Again, considerable reflection has been stimulated by the mentoring role, although without some kind of deliberately set up structure within which these perceptions can be fundamentally addressed and theorised, they may simply remain immediate and possibly only temporary responses which teachers will find very difficult to act on. It may be that the HE institution should take on some kind of role here. It would certainly be possible to build in to mentor training and subject-specific briefing some discussion and consideration of the issues raised by these, and other, reflections.

Marking and assessment, and relating these to National Curriculum levels

Positive

E Mentor conscious of the enormous development in assessment procedures brought about by the National Curriculum, and recognised how difficult this was for students.

E Mentor recognised how much expertise teachers had acquired; both in 'knowing' the unstated criteria operating in assessment procedures, and in speed of marking.

A Mentor made to rethink the value and point of keeping evidence and of completing records.

Negative

D Mentor felt there had been little spin-off here because students needed so much help. She had had to teach students how to recognise potential in pupils for higher achievement, and how to push even the good pupils.

B No real effect, because marking and assessment has been thought out so thoroughly already, and the marking policy is carried out by the whole department.

C No real effect – however, with the student teaching other teachers' classes, Head of Department was able to see what these teachers did about marking.

Comment Some comments here indicate an interestingly 'closed' reaction to the question. Little reference has been made to marking as a formative and diagnostic activity, nor to the practice of marking pupils' work with them. However, mentors did recognise how much expertise they had, and mentor E was very alert to the presence of underlying criteria implicit in much assessment, pointing to those aspects of assessment which remain extremely difficult to define for English. The reaction generally is not one of thinking of changes in practice, but rather one of bringing students up to the level at which teachers operate.

Mentor E also expressed well-developed ideas about how students could be helped to develop their marking expertise, which are obviously the result of her own reflection on marking generally: she suggested that students should be helped to decide on a set of relevant expectations/performance parameters for each class they teach, using these as criteria for marking, rather than blindly attempting to apply mark schemes based entirely on the National Curriculum. Mentor C welcomed the opportunities given her to see how the rest of her department carried out their marking, highlighting the problematic nature of this area of teaching, and the difficulty in always establishing ground rules that will be adhered to.

General

When I first started looking in detail at these responses, I was struck by the many unforced statements which illustrated mentors' need to regenerate their idealism and sense of commitment, and the extent to which they found the annual presence of students a potent stimulus and aid to that end. These statements particularly influenced the way in which I decided to write this report. Each of the five mentors I interviewed held strongly expressed views about the importance of students in their working lives, two of them also expressing their sense of obligation and commitment to future generations of students/teachers. Their need constantly to renew their own idealism and sense of purpose came through in such remarks as 'working with students compensates for lack of team-working within the department', 'the presence of students broadens my own interest in education', 'students are a source of ideas and support'; one mentor wonders how 'she would keep her own commitment going without the annual presence of students'.

In replying generally to the central question, it was clear that all the mentors found themselves prompted into reflection by their interactions with students, and that much of this reflection followed the line of 'reaction, repair, research, retheorising and reformulating' (Griffiths and Tann 1992). In addition to its role as a stimulator to change some practice, the reflection experienced by these mentors appears to have operated as a validator of much of their current practice, a means of reaffirming their own commitment, and, importantly, a way of internalising new ideas and perceptions.

The many other comments made by mentors during these interviews (about the mentor role generally and about students generally, for example) lie outside the scope of this chapter. Their comments about the new system of partnership are, however, pertinent. They recognise the increased workload produced by the mentor role, welcome the closer links with the School of Education, but as mentor E stated, 'school mentors do not see themselves as professional teacher-trainers'. Mentors state in no uncertain terms where their ultimate priorities must lie: 'first responsibility is to the pupils and the running of the department. In any conflict of interest, the students would come second'.

My own feelings are that the current balance operating between the School of Education at Birmingham and partner schools is about right, but that any further devolution of student training to schools will place an insupportable burden on teachers. All the mentors were adamant on one thing: should schools be made responsible for the total training of students, they would feel obliged to withdraw from the scheme.

CHAPTER 3

Residential geography fieldstudy within a partnership framework

The immediacy of studying in the field is often so engaging that the evident result is more permanent learning. People appear to learn best when they are excited, interested and involved. (Pearce 1987, p.36)

The advent of Circular 9/92 has provided further opportunities to broaden the partnership which has traditionally existed between higher education institutions (HEIs) and schools. Within the context of a Geography PGCE course this has served to enhance the quality of initial teacher education of student teachers, as well as the learning of a group of comprehensive school pupils, during a week of residential fieldstudy. This week represents one aspect of the frequent 'school-based' work carried out during the year.

The fieldstudy week can be considered to be a reflection of partnership in its fullest sense. In the period before it starts student teachers liaise with the geography department of the school and receive guidance about the composition and organisation of the fieldwork. Two geography teachers (one an accredited mentor) always accompany their school's pupils during the residential fieldstudy, thus helping to provide support for the student teachers during their first experience of conducting such work. The university tutor acts as an important catalyst in the partnership at each stage of the organisation and running of the week, and as a key figure in the overall initial planning of the activities.

The fieldstudy traditionally takes place during the summer term to capitalise upon the experience students have gained from earlier school placements, and because this is a time when they can undertake fuller planning and teaching responsibilities as a group. Close partnership is obviously essential if such a study is to function to the mutual benefit of all the participants. It is particularly important that the pupils, who in the past have used the data collected during this week to create their GCSE coursework, have a rewarding and positive experience.

The broad social and academic value of fieldstudy has been recognised for some considerable time (Brunsden 1987). Recent writings have served to provide further justification for its inclusion in the study of geography by various ages and abilities of learners (Geographical Association Sixth Form – University Working Group 1984, Hart and Thomas 1986, McPartland and Harvey 1987, Raw 1989, Butt 1994, etc). As an integral component of geography teaching in schools it is therefore essential that some initial teacher education about organising fieldwork is a part of any Geography PGCE course.

The value of fieldstudy is often divided into three specific sections. Firstly the subject-specific contribution relates to the way in which such studies help the learner achieve a deeper understanding of theories, concepts and ideas in geography through contact with the real world. These may have been introduced previously in an abstract or 'disembodied' way in the classroom, with little or no contact with concrete examples in the real world. Thus the inclusion of observational and experimental work in the field – either through hypothesis testing or enquiry fieldwork – acts as a means of reinforcing previously acquired knowledge, skills and understanding. Additionally new areas of study can be introduced for the first time through fieldwork.

Secondly fieldstudy has a student-specific purpose. The benefits of working either in groups or individually outside the classroom may include the creation of self-confidence and a greater sense of enjoyment of the learning process. The team-building nature of much fieldstudy can also enhance interpersonal skills, such as co-operation, flexibility and sensitivity to the needs of others (Smith 1987). Additionally Pearce (1987) observed that learning from direct experience such as fieldwork 'involves participation, commitment and feeling' and 'support(s)...social skills development as well as development in the cognitive and affective domains'.

Lastly fieldstudy, by its very nature, promotes children's understanding and appreciation of the environments around them (Hawkins 1987). It helps them to build an awareness of the need to protect cherished environments and to question forms of development that are not sustainable. 'Awareness and understanding of, and concern and eventual responsibility for, 'real places' can only be achieved through direct contact' (Pearce 1987).

Fieldstudy should no longer be merely of the 'gawk and talk' variety. Lidstone (1988) illustrates the dangers of pupils finding themselves 'in a bind of yet more teacher talk, note-taking and information collecting', whilst teachers suffer the costs of 'preparation, administration...and time spent leaving suitable work for the supply teacher'. Over the last 30 years we have seen the development of different methods of fieldwork ranging from straight field teaching, to field research (positivist, hypothesis testing and deductive), enquiry methods and more humanistic problem solving. Recently more interactive and participatory frameworks have been introduced into fieldstudy which may include elements of values development (Pocock 1983, Hart and Thomas 1987). The learning experiences organised in the field by many geography departments have begun to mirror pupil-centred styles of learning carried out in the classroom. However, it is always important that the style and purpose of the study is educationally sound and that fieldwork is not viewed by teachers as a simple 'panacea' for learning geography.

It is not necessary to revisit the debate about the merits of different styles of fieldwork here. Hall's (1976) overview (Figure 3.1) provides a useful reference if one wishes to make such considerations.

Within the partnership framework of student teachers and children working together during residential fieldstudy the quality of the learning experience of both groups can be enhanced.

Let us consider in turn each of the components of the partnership and see what benefits such fieldstudy can bring.

Fieldstudy as a vehicle for promoting the quality of partnership

Student teachers

For student teachers the chance to organise residential fieldstudy provides a wide range of opportunities to improve the quality of their teaching. One of the main benefits of creating such experience for teachers in training is that they realise 'the pedagogical and organisational complexities of teaching in the field compared to classroom work' (Butt 1994). Appreciating the levels of planning required to organise fieldwork activities which are geographically relevant, involving, challenging and safe – compared to those required to teach effectively in the classroom – is part of the advantage of giving student teachers such responsibility. This is not to imply that teaching in the classroom is necessarily easier or lacking in its own organisational demands, but rather that planning and delivering field teaching is different in many subtle ways. Practicalities concerning the weather, parking facilities, toilets, food, etc, provide their own special organisational challenges!

Many PGCE Geography students also discover that taking part in field activities suggested by their tutor or devised by their peers also teaches them a range of new field techniques. Often students are not aware of

		Process	Type of Structure	Teacher/Pupil	Result
FIELD DEMON-STRATION	(a) Teacher reinforces	In (a) previous classwork is followed up including orientation of map to ground, slope and contours, intervisibility.	Tightly structured linear programme prepared by teacher: 'pause and move on' by foot or vehicle.	Close supervision of class as a class *teacher* – busy leading and talking; *pupils* – passive in (a) and imitative in (b).	Convergent and closed.
	(b) Teacher confronts	In (b) new phenomena and new skills are introduced in the field for the first time. Students record what teacher observes for future classwork or exam study.			
FIELD STUDY	Directed exploration	Pupils highly circumscribed by directives but considerable autonomy of movement. What is discovered, measured, etc, is by teacher intention, but the process is pupil-centred.	Can be fairly tight (i.e. work-sheet of questions) or more loosely phased around a series of guidelines. 'Colonial elephant hunt' where pupils placed advanta-geously to fall over their own environment but shoot their own quarry.	Open supervision with pupils working in groups or individually. Teacher control by effective preparation.	Convergent and closed but room for a margin of personal inference and error.
FIELD TESTING	Controlled inquiry	Research into a specific hypothesis or model along carefully controlled lines in accordance with the conven-tions of deductive science. Problem solving dominant.	Operationally tight (accuracy essential in recording data). Degree of structure and amount of computation a function of hypothesis and techniques employed.	Pupil as researcher and teacher as laboratory supervisor with duty to safeguard data from contamination by irregularities of conduct in research and miscalculations in computation.	Open, unless previously worked out by teacher, or the hypothesis overcontrived by him.
FIELD DISCOVERY	Open inquiry	Journey into the unknown, where theme, guidelines, hypo-thesis, mode of working are the choice of the pupil. 'Discovery', Exploration, Creativity' pos-sible in the widest sense.	Loose, lightly constrained to random.	Only responsibilities of pastoral care, subject consultant by pupil request. Main work is to provide the possibility and encourage inquiry.	Divergent and unpredictable.

Figure 3.1: A simple fieldwork classification in Geography

these different techniques, or have heard or read about them but have not seen them used. It is remarkable how many graduates in Geography who have obtained good degrees and would consider themselves academically capable geographers have never used quadrat sampling techniques in the field, or undertaken stream flow analysis! They are usually well versed in selected quantitative or qualitative techniques (possibly those used in their final year undergraduate dissertations) but beyond these have only a cursory appreciation of the diversity of field techniques that can be used with children.

Another important facet of conducting residential fieldstudy is that the student teachers' appreciation of its importance within geography education is reinforced. Fieldstudy is an entitlement for children throughout the key stages (see the current Geography National Curriculum (DES 1991a) and the School Curriculum and Assessment Authority's draft proposals for Geography (SCAA 1994)) and is a compulsory part of virtually all GCSEs, A and AS levels in Geography. Its academic importance should therefore be stressed throughout initial teacher education. As Bailey (1974) stated, fieldwork is a necessary part of geographical education; it is not an optional extra.

Realising the kinds of pressures that fieldwork is under in schools with regard to curriculum time and resources is similarly important. Beginning teachers need to know that they should be prepared to 'fight their corner' over fieldstudy, for they are teaching at a time of reduced resources, increased costs, changes in curricular focus and priorities, and debate regarding the safety of fieldwork and outdoor activities. Interestingly Lidstone (1988) highlights the problem that fieldwork is often regarded by other subject teachers as a separate undertaking from 'normal' geography taught in the classroom. This misconception should be countered, Lidstone suggests, by geography teachers clarifying that fieldwork is a '*sine qua non* of all good education through geography'.

University tutor

For the university tutor the partnership of student teachers, mentor teachers and children working together is a fruitful one. The quality of student teachers' work and of partnership is increased on a variety of levels – student teachers generally improve their integration within their group of peers and develop both individual and team teaching skills. This development may not have been forthcoming either before or during teaching practices in schools. Often students find the tasks of planning and teaching in a team difficult, and the field course provides a good opportunity to enhance this in a supported way. For the tutor this is probably one of the few chances to see the students working together with children for any sustained period of time.

The tutor also has an opportunity to promote the concepts and workings of partnership. The space to do this during the year may have been rather limited, for although the tutor regularly works with students in groups or individually, and with mentor teachers in a similar way, he or she has relatively few opportunities to combine all of these partnership elements in a teaching context. With the number of visits made by tutors to schools to observe students teach severely reduced, such 'triangles' of contact are disappearing; this unfortunately is of little benefit to anyone. During residential fieldstudy all the components of partnership are jointly functioning, with the tutor on hand to direct and develop the model of partnership which seems most appropriate. In the early period of partnership under Circular 9/92 the chance to work in this way is obviously welcomed by all concerned.

An additional benefit for the tutor is the chance to gather further 'recent and relevant' experience of working with, and teaching, children. The inevitable time restrictions of life within universities are often keenly felt by tutors, who therefore welcome the opportunity to spend time with children in the context of residential fieldstudy.

Mentor teachers

The benefits to the university tutor and Geography PGCE students in training are therefore numerous – but what do a partnership school, its geography department and most importantly the pupils gain from the arrangements?

In organisational terms the partnership school should find itself in a position where the students and the tutor from the HE institution take the lead. This may involve some early negotiations between the school and HEI on the location for the fieldstudy, costs involved, and number of pupils to be taken, but after that (apart from the usual internal arrangements made by the school for any field trip such as collecting money, consent forms, arranging transport, etc) the rest can almost be left to the student teachers and tutor. As part of the student teachers' training the HEI may wish to give them selected responsibility for booking accommodation, arranging transport, etc, and will certainly want them to try to select fieldstudy sites and techniques to be used with the children. Here the school has an important initial input in informing the HEI of their specific requirements, for example with respect to the pupils' coursework or syllabus needs.

Mentor teachers have a role in the overall functioning of the week for they provide another link between the school, its pupils and the PGCE students. Knowing the pastoral and academic strengths and weaknesses of the group of children, as well as any management or behavioural issues that may arise, the teachers are invaluable as a resource. However, their responsibilities are perhaps not as taxing as on 'ordinary' field courses, where teachers are usually the sole arbiters of pupil behaviour, organisation, and field activities. On this study they will be helping to advise the student teachers in concert with the university tutor who has a fuller appreciation of the range of different students' capabilities.

The ratio of 'teachers' to pupils is also generous for the children are not now accompanied by only two or three members of staff, but also by a group of student teachers as well. The simple fact of having more hands to work with the pupils makes everyone's teaching commitments easier.

Pupils

The major advantage for the children is the individualised attention which they receive at most times when they are in learning situations due to the greater number of teachers (student teachers, mentor teachers, university tutor) available to assist and guide them. Such support is very rare in day to day teaching in the maintained sector, indeed the children may never have experienced similar ratios before and may never again. The plethora of adults actually helps to create a more relaxed atmosphere – the children are not subdued by the greater number of teachers, and indeed often comment in their evaluations that they did not realise that teachers could be such 'fun' or behave like 'real people'.

Case Study – A residential field course in Coniston

To illustrate how fieldstudy can enhance the quality of partnership and the learning experiences of student teachers and pupils, it is worthwhile considering a case study of a week's residential fieldstudy undertaken each summer by the Geography PGCE students at the University of Birmingham. The students are directed to organise this fieldstudy using a named local partnership comprehensive school in Birmingham. The location of the study is usually the university's outdoor education centre at Coniston Water in the Lake District.

Student teachers either organise themselves, or are organised, into their own groups for the week. In the interests of fairness (and speed!) it is often best for the tutor to undertake this task, randomly selecting groups of students into twos or threes. These groups are told that their abilities to work together as a team when setting up, delivering and debriefing the fieldwork will be assessed. Just as in schools where not all staff members see 'eye to eye' this is equally true of students in training. It is therefore prudent for the tutor to slightly engineer groupings if necessary; although a broad ability to work professionally with colleagues is always important and should be developed as part of this week. As Raw (1989) suggests, 'success depends on the willingness of colleagues to co-operate in a common goal'.

The preplanning for the fieldstudy is considerable and although the students do not necessarily have to consider, say, the booking of the centre or the financial arrangements, they are responsible for virtually all the day to day organisation of the week itself. They have to co-ordinate and lead the field activities, briefing and debriefing of pupils, work sessions in the evenings, cooking, cleaning and any 'entertainments' for the pupils (such as table tennis competitions run in the evening). Students are made aware that it is their individual and collective responsibility to 'run' the fieldstudy during the week, with their tutor and teachers acting in an advisory role.

Early in the summer term (the fieldstudy usually takes place within the first two weeks of May) the student teachers are prompted by their tutor to arrange a meeting with the geography teachers from the partnership school. The teachers are invited into the university for a session where they brief the students about the group of children who are being taken on the fieldstudy (often Year 10) and the proposed geographical content of the week. This establishes the GCSE syllabus that the children are following, what aspects of the syllabus have been covered already, the requirements of fieldwork-based coursework and therefore the parameters of the fieldstudy that might be undertaken in the Lake District. Some tutor guidance is often required at this stage to achieve overall balance and structure for the week. The meeting also deals with such practicalities as pupils' names and medical requirements, friendship groups and 'social' information used in the composition of working groups for the children.

One major difficulty for the students trying to plan actual field methods at this stage is that they are working 'blind', basing their selection of possible fieldsites and techniques either on previous experience of the Lakes, or map extracts. This problem can be overcome, in part, by the mentor teacher and tutor suggesting certain locations to explore the overarching theme for the week (in this case 'Human impacts and conflicts of interest in a National Park'). Students then organise resources and worksheets – which may need amending later – and are reminded of the need to visit their sites before the pupils undertake any fieldwork. These site visits are used to assess whether the students' activities will work, to collect further resources, to check on parking facilities and toilets and to ensure that the location is safe. They take place under the guidance of the university tutor before the pupils and teachers arrive. Again the tutor has a major responsibility here, for it is not seen as helpful to use student selected fieldsites, activities or worksheets if these are not pedagogically or geographically sound.

A typical field week planned by the students might be structured as shown in Figure 3.2.

The pupils' views – questionnaires completed at the end of the fieldstudy

As a means of evaluating the quality of the work undertaken during the fieldstudy the student teachers usually want to gain some feedback from the pupils they have taught. This is partly gathered on a daily basis from individuals and groups during the course of the work undertaken – however a slightly more formal and organised 'feedback' is helpful.

To gather this information some student teachers have previously devised a small and simple questionnaire for the pupils to be completed on their last evening. The following is an example of such a questionnaire used with a group of 21 (12 boys, 9 girls) Year 10 pupils taking GCSE Geography.

---

1. What did you enjoy doing most during the fieldstudy?

2. Why did you enjoy this?

3. What would you like to do again?

4. What fieldstudy skills do you think you have developed that have been most useful to you?

5. What did you find most difficult?

Any additional comments?

The overall tone and nature of the statements made by the pupils illustrate two important findings; firstly that they felt that their geographical knowledge and understanding improved during the fieldstudy, and secondly that they had enjoyed the overall experience. As many educational theorists have postulated, these two things are not unconnected.

Of the 21 pupils sampled most were extremely positive about the field course, indeed 3 respondents stated that they had enjoyed 'everything' (2)

FIELD COURSE (Sunday to Friday) Overall theme of fieldwork: 'Human impact and conflict of interest within a National Park'

Sunday	Monday	Tuesday	Wednesday	Thursday	Friday
10.00am: Student teachers and tutor leave Birmingham.	8.15am: Breakfast.	8.15am: Breakfast.	8.15am: Breakfast.	8.15am: Breakfast.	8.15am: Breakfast.
	9.00am: Site visits.	9.30am: GROUP 2: *Langdale Valley, Stickle Tarn:* Glaciation study.	9.30am: GROUP 3: *Windermere:* A tourism centre.	9.30am: GROUP 4: *Langdale Valley:* Land use and human impact.	9.30am: GROUP 5: *Hawkshead:* Village study.
1.00pm: Arrive at fieldstudy centre. Site visits.	10.00am: Return to fieldstudy centre.		1.00pm: Grizedale Forest. Conflicts of interest in forestry.	*OR*	1.00pm: Depart Hawkshead.
	2.00pm: Partnership school and mentor teachers arrive. GROUP 1: *Lake shore walk:* Leisure centre siting exercise. Coniston.			Sellafield and St. Bees Head. Nuclear energy and coastal study.	
6.00pm: Return to fieldstudy centre. Discuss further site visits.	5.30pm: Return to fieldstudy centre. GROUP 1: *debrief.*	5.30pm: Return to fieldstudy centre. GROUP 2: *debrief.*	5.30pm: Return to fieldstudy centre. GROUP 3: *debrief.*	5.30pm: Return to fieldstudy centre. GROUP 4: *debrief.*	GROUP 5: *debrief.* 5.00pm: Arrive Birmingham.
	7.15pm: Meal.	7.15pm: Meal.	7.15pm: Meal.	7.15pm: Meal.	
8.00pm: Meal.	8.00pm: Evening work (all pupils and students).	8.00pm: Evening work (all pupils and students).	8.00pm: Evening work (all pupils and students).	8.00pm: Evening work (all pupils and students).	
	10.30pm: To rooms.	10.30pm: To rooms.	10.30pm: To rooms.	10.30pm: To rooms.	

Figure 3.2

or 'all of it' (1) in response to question 1. Other responses varied quite widely – although most stated that they had enjoyed walking the Langdale valley (12), some tempered this by saying that walking down had been better than walking up (4)! Often pupils responded that they had enjoyed visiting Sellafield (4), St Bees Head (3), or Grizedale Forest (3), also mentioning field activities that they had carried out at these sites.

Some comments were directly linked to geographical education ('I enjoyed the car park survey and questionnaires', 'doing the coastal transect', 'the Sellafield centre was well designed and got me thinking about a highly controversial issue'), whilst others emphasised the social and recreational activities that took place at some time during the days ('playing football', 'good social atmosphere', 'the slides at Grizedale centre', and 'table tennis in the evening').

Asked why they had enjoyed these activities and locations (question 2) the responses were diverse. Those who had cited Langdale valley as their most enjoyable day had usually been affected by the surrounding environment and favourable weather conditions at the time ('cool streams and a well spread out landscape', 'I liked the valley trip because it was a new and different experience for me', 'the water in the rivers was refreshing', 'the scenery was gorgeous and I got to see some glacial features', 'it was warm and downhill', 'the Langdale walk was on a nice day so enabling me to wade in the Tarn'). Others mentioned skills they had learned at different locations (3), or just that the day they chose had been 'fun'(4) or 'interesting' (5).

Very occasionally pupils would focus directly on the benefits for their Geography GCSE – 'I thought it was very interesting work and brilliant for my coursework'. The fact that this only rarely occurred raises an interesting parallel point – there is considerable evidence that although pupils may find the process of making the link between fieldwork and coursework possible, their use of field examples in written examinations is extremely limited. Lidstone (1988) suggests that fieldwork may be just too 'distinctive' from either class-based or other examination work for the link to be made; whilst McPartland and Harvey (1987) noted that at a research conference involving teachers and lecturers who promoted fieldwork 'none of the participants…saw the purpose of fieldwork in the more utilitarian terms of assisting students and pupils in passing their final examinations'.

In response to question 3 most children wanted to repeat again the activities that they had enjoyed most (see responses to question 1).

The fieldstudy skills that pupils felt had been most helpful to them (question 4) were varied and often correlated to the days they felt had been most enjoyable. Notable amongst these were fieldsketches (6), questionnaire work (4), transects (3), and using clinometers (3). Some responses joined together the skills with the geographical content of days, creating a number of responses which state things like 'glaciation skills' or 'forestry work skills'. This possibly highlights a potential problem that pupils see these skills as relating solely to this geographical context, and not as 'generic' skills that can be applied elsewhere.

Question 5, which enquired about the difficulties pupils had faced, was poorly answered. This may be a good sign suggesting that pupils were supported so well that difficulties had not arisen. The one common problem that pupils appeared to have was related to fieldsketching.

The section of additional comments was generally helpful and, in some instances, amusing. Pupils who had found the Langdale valley exercises difficult gave helpful advice ('split the party into two and have a fast and slow group'), whilst those who had trouble with the questionnaire surveys suggested possible reasons ('the people at the car park were *so* grumpy!') Many comments were highly supportive of the week containing positive references to the social atmosphere that had prevailed – 'the teachers were brilliant and friendly', 'I have had a really good week and have enjoyed the general good spirit of the group', 'the students were great – they didn't play the role of 'teacher' too much and were more like friends – *thanks*. I had a great time!', 'the students were brill and it was great fun' (14 comments).

Although only mentioned directly by two pupils there was a feeling that some evening work sessions had been too long, especially if they extended beyond ten o'clock at night. In this respect the student teachers were often more vocal than the pupils with their concerns!

Finally the disruption to normal sleeping patterns that is often associated with residential fieldstudy was mentioned by certain pupils – 'I didn't find anything difficult, except getting to sleep', 'if I was a student teacher I wouldn't make us get up at 8 o'clock' and the need for 'more flexible sleeping hours' were three such comments!

The student teachers' views

The student teachers' end of course evaluations of the entire PGCE in Geography regularly make positive, and unsolicited, reference to the residential fieldstudy undertaken with a partnership school. This, in part, is almost certainly because students generally enjoy this type of geographical activity anyway and are again working together as an entire method group. However, they clearly also perceive the opportunities that fieldstudy offers to improve their teaching abilities and develop their powers of self-analysis and reflection. The assessment of practical and organisational skills associated with the fieldstudy is highly valued, for it is far removed from the narrow, theoretical and 'library-based' work that many government critics wrongly attribute to teacher education courses.

Comments made by the students highlight the importance they place upon a fieldstudy component within the course:

'The range of experiences in schools, in the classroom and in the field provided me with a sound basis from which to move my ideas forward.'

'The structure of the course was excellent, mixing a blend of lecture/activity/field courses which were enjoyable.'

Other comments focus upon the development of skills, resources, teaching experiences and opportunities for personal development that fieldstudy offers:

'The fieldstudy helped me develop teaching skills even though I was no longer on teaching practice.'

'The fieldwork was enjoyable and productive which gave me a range of resources useful for further trips.'

'Fieldwork was excellent, both an enjoyable and very valuable experience for me as a teacher.'

'Personal development? – probably on the field course! This was an excellent week combining theory, practice and fun.'

In addition students often comment positively upon the novelty of being observed by their peers as they teach in the field or at the fieldcentre, for this observation provides a range of points for discussion and can suggest new teaching techniques to try. These techniques can be discussed with other students, the university tutor or the teachers at the time. The desire to prove one's competence in front of a group of fellow students is also a strong performance motivator, although initially some find the experience rather daunting.

Conclusions

Many Geography ITT courses include fieldwork within their schemes of work, but the number that can arrange residential work with children and a mentor teacher in attendance are perhaps not great in number. The advantages in promoting quality of educational experiences for all concerned are apparent, particularly so due to the levels of support that are available at all stages of the process. Those schools who eventually employ student teachers trained in this way are therefore placed at an advantage.

The roles and responsibilities of the pupils, students, teachers and tutor during the fieldstudy are all important and complementary, but ultimately different. There is little doubt that such a field course could be run within a wholly school-centred model of training – but it would certainly not afford the breadth of benefits that a partnership model allows. The university tutor has a unique appreciation of each student teachers' strengths and weaknesses and an immediate concern for their continuing development. Teachers, including mentors, who accompany their school's children on fieldstudy have a very different focus. Their primacy of concern, quite rightly, has to be for the children, not the student teachers. In short the partnership model is successful in delivering quality of educational experience for both students and pupils precisely because of the variations in the roles adopted by the tutor and teachers.

CHAPTER 4

Partnership in History: the use of site visits

In the PGCE history partnership with schools at Birmingham University tutors and mentors try to find ways of working together which will utilise best the skills and expertise of both sides to the advantage of each other. In the autumn term group visits are made to schools when new students learn much, practising their new ideas under the watchful eyes of experienced teachers; in the summer term students use their much increased confidence and skills to the benefit of schools. One of the most successful examples of this is to be seen in the work done on site visits. This chapter is based on action research, describing and analysing our practice in this area. The views of some of the participants are also used to gauge the quality of what is done.

In the present National Curriculum Order for history, site visits are a statutory requirement at each key stage (DES 1991b, pp.14, 16, 34). More importantly perhaps, they have long been recognised by history teachers as a lively and stimulating method of helping pupils to understand the past better and engage in active historical enquiry whatever their age or level of ability. In the current frenetic educational climate, however, with schools anxious to perform well in Standard Assessment Tasks (SATs) and League Tables and for OFSTED, it is not always easy to justify disrupting the timetable by taking children and the necessary accompanying staff out of school. This is particularly so in the case of non-examination work for a non-core subject. The problem is compounded by the regulation that schools can no longer demand that parents pay for school visits which take place in school-time. Schools can get round this problem by carefully worded letters to parents and help to needy cases but the cost of covering for the number of staff needed to supervise a trip is heavy.

One of the ways in which higher education can help partnership schools in initial teacher training to overcome the difficulties in meeting their statutory obligations on site visits in history is by supplying student teachers to run the visits. At the University of Birmingham we have a long history of doing this, much longer indeed than the life of the National Curriculum or Circular 9/92 criteria. Back in the 1980s the PGCE history tutors had developed a scheme whereby their main subject students for that year taught the lessons for an entire year group in a Birmingham school over a period of four weeks. The focal point of these four weeks was a site visit: the lessons beforehand prepared the pupils for this whilst those after followed up what they had done on it. Since 1989 I have continued this custom, in particular, since 1992, building up a close partnership with Broadway School, a mixed, inner city comprehensive which has regularly given teaching placements to students and whose senior management take pride in the work they do with both students and newly qualified teachers. In 1992 we (that is, university tutors and students) took Broadway's Year 9 to the Black Country Museum; in 1993 and 1994 we took Year 7 to Kenilworth Castle.

The nature of the whole enterprise has subtly changed over the years with Andy Wainwright, the head of the history department at Broadway and myself working out how to integrate the work done into the whole history curriculum rather than it being merely an interesting adjunct. Thus the choice of Kenilworth Castle for the department teaches about castles as their supplementary study unit A (a unit which extends the study of the core British study units for this key stage) and as part of core study unit 2, Medieval Realms: Britain 1066 to 1500, in KS3 (DES 1991b, pp.39, 47).

Organisation and preparation

The organisation for the visits – there were so many pupils we had to spread the visits over two days – were shared between the school who were responsible for the practical arrangements and the university who provided the teaching and resources. Andy Wainwright first cleared the arrangements with the senior management of the school who have, indeed, been supportive of the collaboration with the university from the beginning and increasingly so each year. With their blessing, Andy prepared a missive for the staff which detailed briefly the history of this partnership, the objects of the exercise and the arrangements for the students coming into school. He ended with spelling out the advantages to Broadway which he saw as: (i) the pupils being enabled to visit Kenilworth Castle for a whole day (before collaborating with the university only half a day could be managed); (ii) Broadway staff benefiting (both by students running the visit so that non-history staff do not have to take time out of lessons to accompany the visit or to cover the lessons of those who do, and by students taking lessons in a very busy month in the teaching calendar); (iii) pupils being taught over four weeks in relatively small groups; and (iv) a continuation and development of the school's special links with the university.

Andy also booked us in at Kenilworth, organised the buses, sent letters to parents and saw to the financial matters including, of course, the pupils' contributions which are subsidised by money built especially into the history account. Since Kenilworth is an English Heritage site the site visit itself is free. All these arrangements were made in close liaison with the university, the dates of the visit especially having to dovetail with the PGCE timetable.

It was not so easy matching the school's lesson timetable with that of the students. In theory one morning's seminar a week was devoted to the time in school but since the eight Year 7 classes were taught over four days, in practice working out which groups of students were free to attend them was somewhat difficult. In 1993 fathoming out how to do this severely taxed the brains of both teacher and tutors: in 1994 we handed this task over to the two students who had been at Broadway for teaching practice and all was sorted out in five minutes! Clearly at this stage in the year there are benefits to all in using the talents of nearly qualified teachers.

Through Andy Wainwright and the students who already know the school, much valuable information was gleaned about the pupils themselves, what they had already studied and what understanding and skills we might expect from them. At the university, the first session of the summer term was devoted to an exploration of what use site visits have for both pupils in school and history students on initial teacher training courses. The advantages of using visual source material, seeing history in concrete terms, putting knowledge in context, stimulating enquiry, investigation and roleplay and enabling oral, group and cross-curricular work were quickly pointed out by the students. Those of developing concepts, empathy and an aesthetic sense, taking opportunities for different methods of presentation and meeting the National Curriculum programmes of study (PoS), including the attainment targets (ATs), took a little longer to tease out but, after discussion, were easily added to the list. It was readily seen that since all site work is based automatically on the use of sources, all the strands of AT3 (the use of historical sources) could be met by thoughtful planning of appropriate tasks and enquiries. Similarly, all sites give evidence of features of the past (AT1c) and most demonstrate change over time (AT1a). A useful dimension that took longer to work out was that of using historical remains and reconstruction for work on interpretation thus overcoming many of the perceived difficulties of AT2 – interpretations of history. Above all, we decided that site visits gave the opportunity for pupil-centred learning, excitement and fun. The concept of serendipity, new to many students, was added to our list of advantages.

The advantages to the students themselves are obviously central to this project. Since site visits are a statutory requirement history students must have some education in the purpose of them and how to run them. A particular advantage of spending time on them in ITE is that students can improve their own skills in using concrete evidence in teaching to the ATs, developing historical skills in pupils and encouraging pupil-centred learning. For us the great advantage in doing them in the summer term is that the students have already done a short-term and a long-term placement in schools and thus have the opportunity to put their experience and expertise together, sharing their newly developed skills in varied group work and team teaching. Most of them were to confess that doing so put them on their mettle but also allowed them explore fresh ideas and methods of teaching and learning.

The students also had the chance, obviously, to learn from the expertise of the teachers at Broadway, not least in the important skills of organisation and management of school visits. We did spend some time at the university on the practical side of site visits, including the necessary advice on lavatories, waterproof clothing and sick-bags although the students did not know whether to be glad or sorry when the latter two in turn proved to be vital.

The history department at Broadway had suggested some ways in which the students might focus on the work to be done at Kenilworth. Changes in castle building between 1100 and 1600 and how castles were defended and attacked were the chief suggestions made but the students were left fairly free to make best use of the site. Following from the experience of the previous year (Watts 1993, *Welsh Historian*, pp.15–18) I had decided that some history teaching on castles and an investigation of materials on Kenilworth Castle to see how it could be used to develop pupils' understanding of castles would be fruitful. Degree courses in history do not usually teach students the type of details about castles they need for teaching twelve-year-olds so many of our students found the resources supplied quite fascinating. These resources included Schools History Project (SHP) *Contrasts and Connections* (with the teaching handbook) as this was the textbook used at Broadway, SHP *Castles and Cathedrals* and various other of the new textbooks which have been published on this since the advent of the National Curriculum, a range of English Heritage materials including a copy of its teaching book on Kenilworth Castle for each group and various other relevant books and visual aids.

This preparatory work was particularly important as this year, because of timetabling difficulties, some of the students had to meet and teach their pupils for the first time before they visited Kenilworth Castle. This was not ideal although the students coped very well. The visit itself helped to develop the students' own understanding of the site and its history considerably. The twenty-six students were divided into three groups and, in turn, attempted to answer a pupils' workbook from the year before, explore the site on their own and go round it with Sylvia Pinches, a local historian with a particular interest in Kenilworth. The purpose of answering the workbook was to think about what the best type of work-sheets might be as well as having a chance to empathise with pupils who are given such tasks so often. The use of a local historian was invaluable in acquiring accurate and interesting information although those students who had wandered around looking for themselves before their guided tours were most alive to thinking about the uses of the different parts of the castle – a useful fact to remember for the future and to consider in planning activities for the pupils. After an hour and a half the students gathered in their groups to discuss with tutors the possibilities of the site for KS3 work on castles, how cross-curricular links could be made, what resources were available, how the pupils should be organised and cared for on the day, how the work should be timed and what alternative strategies there should be in case of bad weather. How materials should be presented with attention to language, clarity, coherence and interest were also important considerations as was the overriding one that pupils should have fun and enjoy their visit to an historic site.

Further consideration could be given to such points when the students went into the school as then they could find out from their own experience and from the history staff what their pupils were like and of what they were capable. It is only from working with actual pupils in such a way that students can put their ideas in context. Equally, schools gain because it is difficult for staff to spend so much time on preparation or certainly to have so many minds all bent to the same consideration.

The staff were able to help the students on what the pupils had already studied – chiefly the Norman Conquest and feudalism – and what was the general level of achievement in each class. The classes were banded but throughout special attention was given to language since Broadway is a multi-ethnic school and some pupils speak English as a second language. Guidance from the staff on this was particularly useful for those of our students whose teaching experience had been in rather different schools, although differentiated and special needs teaching is part of our course.

Preparatory lessons

The first lessons at Broadway enabled the students to introduce themselves and get to know their pupils. Six of the classes had three students to teach them and two had four. The pupils responded exceedingly well to such a staff/pupil ratio and as in such group visits to schools earlier in the academic year, staff were wryly happy to see what can be achieved in such auspicious circumstances. The students took advantage of their numbers in various ways, some team teaching, others teaching the pupils in small groups or using a mixture of such methods. They explored what their pupils already knew or understood about castles and built upon this to prepare them for Kenilworth. Many of them used various visual exercises to build up understanding of motte and bailey castles and how castles might develop from there: some used specific materials on Kenilworth so that their pupils might have a framework into which to fit their experiences on the visit. Very importantly, they also used various strategies to learn the names of their pupils and begin to form a working relationship with them.

Much of the work for this first visit had to be prepared in the students' own time although seminar time was given for the preparatory work for the visit to Kenilworth itself. Although the school was happy for the students to use its photocopying facilities, of necessity most of such work was done at the university and over the next few weeks all the paraphernalia of preparing visual aids, worksheets and booklets, including scissors, glue and acetate sheets were in constant demand.

The site visits

On the two days of the site visits the students whose classes were going that day met early at the school so that they could accompany the children on the buses, thus relieving the school of the necessity to release any more staff for this other than two history teachers and, on one day, a special needs teacher who worked closely with some of the pupils. The high number of student teachers helped gentle containment of the pupils as great excitement abounded, many of them not having gone to such a place before.

The value of having so many 'teachers' was easily visible from the start. Each day four classes were taken around the castle but each was doing something different. All the classes had specially devised booklets of varying lengths, with maps, pictures and plans. The booklets varied in style, however – some were hand-drawn, some relied on photocopied pictures. They also had very different activities and in the course of their visits pupils were engaged in observing, finding, measuring, drawing, writing, planning methods of attack and defence, roleplay, empathy exercises, stories, games and a whole host of oral enquiries.

The classes were organised differently too – some students choosing to keep all their class together although with each student being responsible for specific pupils; others divided their classes into groups throughout the day and went around in small groups. On both days some students adapted their organisation according to how the pupils best responded. One very lively class, for example, settled down better when divided up; another, rather less quick usually in their historical understanding, conversely came to life when kept together as a class but engaged in very active learning in the Great Hall of John of Gaunt by four energetic (and later, totally exhausted) students. In another case one student kept just three boys with her all the time, thus allowing them to develop their ideas at their own pace and achieve at a higher level than was normally possible. Such flexibility is not usually open to teachers on a site visit. It was used here to enable much differentiated learning – always a potential bonus in active learning anyway.

Student styles of teaching varied enormously too – from Steve who brilliantly used his charismatic manner, prepared plans and a focal point at the centre of the castle to enable his class to point accurately *en masse* to whichever of the three main building areas he referred, to others like Jason and Charlotte who quietly chatted to and gently probed the minds of their groups. It was easy to perceive that whether the pupils were working in a very close relationship with one student or being fired with excitement like Lisa, Graham and Lesley's class who charged off to find the gardens *en masse*, the students running desperately behind them, that they were thoroughly enjoying themselves. They were involved in historical enquiry and wanting to discover more whilst developing social skills at the same time.

Such enthusiasm was not dampened by the rain on the first visit although the class which had chosen to examine the castle defences from walking around the outside of the walls got soaked. Contingency plans had been made and between the use of the education room and having an early lunch on the buses, disaster was averted. Student numbers and quick thinking were of use here both in finding all kinds of sheltered corners in the castle where one student and a few pupils could continue their investigations and in helping the enclosed lunch to remain orderly and cheerful. As Andy Wainwright remarked, 'The way the students used the double-decker buses as a resource and turned the decks into classrooms was excellent.'

The teachers from Broadway were able to wander around and join in where and when they saw fit. Andy was able to devote his energy at appropriate times of each day to ensuring order in the small castle shop and both staff and tutors were free to help any pupil or student who needed them at any moment. The students proved more than equal to any contingency, however, and, both at Kenilworth and in the ensuing weeks, the Broadway staff were happy to let them take charge.

Follow-up lessons

The following week we spent a session reflecting on what we had done so far and where and how we might improve what we were doing. As usual on our course it was the interplay of ideas and suggestions which led to the most fruitful results. There had already been feedback after lessons and on site and now the students could pool their experiences and share any worries. They had jelled together in their groups although different approaches to teaching had led to some strong, if friendly, arguments on the way. Their understanding of their pupils had grown, especially on the site visits, and this allowed them to plan the next two weeks' work with increasing confidence, particularly in respect to the needs and abilities of the children.

The ensuing weeks saw a continuation of the variety of approach and individual attention to pupils and their progression. The students excelled themselves in producing varying resources, proving that their computer skills had increased enormously from the beginning of the course too. Pictures, plans, diagrams, stories were utilised to stimulate the pupils to reply in kind. DART (directed activities related to the text) strategies, differentiated worksheets, open-ended tasks were used to help the varying capacities of the children. The chief resource, however, was obviously going to be the pupils themselves and their experiences of Kenilworth.

Following through their previous work, students concentrated on developing the concept of change over time – Kenilworth's massive Norman keep, graceful John of Gaunt apartments and splendid Elizabethan buildings offering a marvellous example of this – or looking at both aspects of the castle as a fortified home or taking one of the historic moments in the life of Kenilworth Castle to explore that period of its history in greater depth. Simon de Montfort's rebellion in 1266 and Queen Elizabeth's visit to Leicester's home were the favourite stories for the latter approach. Two classes used a story of an attack on the castle to generate interest both in the different attitudes of the people involved in the politics of thirteenth century warfare and in the ways they could attack and defend castles. Certainly all the attainment targets were covered, including AT2, as were many aspects of the programme of study. Roleplay, cartoons, posters, tourist guides, group collages were amongst the different ways pupils were stimulated to communicate the results of their investigations. Students structured or set up open-ended tasks according to the needs of their pupils.

The students, once again, organised their classes in various ways appropriate to the nature of the work they were doing or the preferences of the students. Some preferred team teaching in which they were steadily growing more proficient, others divided into groups throughout although these groups might or might not be all engaged on the same task. In some classes work had been deliberately organised so that the total picture would only be seen when all the groups put their displays together. By the end of the fortnight history rooms were covered in the various displays so that pupils in Year 7 could see how their peers had responded to the visit to Kenilworth as well as taking pride in their own efforts.

The advantages of partnership

The pupils, indeed, reacted very positively to the whole project: Andy Wainwright believed that this was partly because it was a totally different experience for them and that they could focus well on their investigations and activities because these were based on what they had seen for themselves. Small group work was particularly good for the less able, some of whom like to 'cling' to their teachers, but it also served to channel the liveliness of the brighter pupils who were usually taught in bigger classes where it might be difficult to give them the individual attention which they too need. Discipline was certainly easier with so many teachers around: in fact, the headteacher was very pleased to have the unusual satisfaction for any school of the bus company telephoning him to congratulate him on the general behaviour of the pupils whilst on their buses.

Both on the site visit itself and in the classroom the staff were pleased by the students' quick grasp of what was appropriate for their children and the ensuing variety of activities in which they engaged them. They were also happy that the work integrated so well into their KS3 syllabus and that all the ATs were covered, Kenilworth, as Andy Wainwright said, being peculiarly 'open for source work and change'. He liked the students' good use of stories, their ways of making development over time clear visually and, most important of all, the fact that 'a lot of good history was taught'.

For the staff there were obvious advantages if only as Andy remarked, 'From a purely selfish point of view, students do all the work. We can return from a site visit feeling relaxed. Once we are actually there we are absolved from care' – a happy state in which to be with their pupils and which must affect both favourably.

The students themselves picked up much on this latter point. Helen, for example, hoped that their month's teaching helped the teachers to feel 'fresher and more relaxed' at a particularly busy time. Alistair, Jason, Lesley and others trusted that the fact that the students had the luxury of more time to prepare for a site visit than 'overworked and underpaid' staff paid dividends in lively, varied work and resources. Many students tentatively hoped that, just as they had learnt much from the teachers, perhaps the latter had picked up some new ideas from them. All of the students were very aware of the enormous potential of a high teacher/pupils ratio.

The advantages to the students in doing this work was amply demonstrated in their energetic (sometimes frenetic) co-operative labours in planning, organising and teaching. When later they reflected on the whole project, they agreed that it had been very worthwhile, teaching them much about the organisation of school trips and how to use a site visit for stimulating good learning and a lot of interest and fun in history. Joy probably spoke for others when she added, 'My understanding of how castles were built has improved from nil to good now!' Most of the students certainly would have preferred a day rather than half a day at Kenilworth before they started teaching and this will be put into the future programme as, hopefully will other suggested improvements such as the school providing an ion camera, and the need for religious dates, which cost some of our students a lesson, to be given to the university beforehand. Overwhelmingly, however, the whole exercise was praised by the students. As Tim Amann explained, he now felt confident he knew how to plan and organise a site visit and, in particular, how to use an historic building to develop historical understanding and skills in schoolchildren. He felt he had learnt new skills himself and new methods through working with the other students and in a different school, but that the whole exercise showed how to stimulate creative thinking about the purpose of building and, without using complex language, help pupils to think in inventive terms and respond well to open-ended teaching.

Such skills were to be demonstrated later in the term when we took Year 9 of Park View, a mixed inner city comprehensive school, to the Black Country Museum and when the students produced their study packs on a National Curriculum study unit at the end of the year. Each of these had to incorporate a site visit into whichever study unit they had chosen and the general standard of imaginative, intelligently planned, stimulating examples which were produced repaid amply the amount of work which had gone into the whole enterprise. It demonstrated the students' capacity to use and reflect upon their experiences and incorporate them into a holistic conception of what good history teaching is about.

In conclusion, through collaborating with a partnership school in this way the needs of both partners are met. The students developed their expertise as teachers in a truly integrated university/school-based course whilst enabling a whole year of a secondary school to enjoy a site visit and a month of lessons in which they could be given much individual attention. Statutory requirements were met and days out from school arranged with far less cost for cover or staff time than usual. Fresh ideas and long experience were able to unite in a teaching adventure enjoyed by all. As Andy Wainwright said, 'The only negative reaction of the pupils was "Why didn't it last longer?"'.

CHAPTER 5

Partnership in Science: IT in science education

Introduction

As with the other kinds of knowledge, skills and confidence which students are expected to develop during their PGCE course, knowledge, skills and confidence in the IT aspects of science education cannot be developed entirely as a result of a *training* process, largely because there is insufficient time in the course for this. Instead, the course places great reliance on an *educative* process in which the student's development is not only progressive, but also dependent on their own effort and thinking.

In principle, both training and education can be provided by means of partnership between schools and the School of Education. However, the model of partnership which requires that each of the partners providing the process is equally capable of doing so is inappropriate as far as IT is concerned since there is much evidence of the relatively low rate of development of IT in schools (Passey and Ridgway 1994).

This chapter describes an example of an alternative model of partnership in which expertise was not evenly shared. In this case the expertise was provided by the staff and students of the School of Education, and the schools provided a context in which the students' skills could be developed. This was, however, not merely a passive role since the context for the work was a problem identified by the schools, followed by continual appraisal of the solutions as they developed. Inevitably, the descriptions of the problems, and the proposed solutions tend to be rather technical. For this reason, and the need to understand the overall learning process of which this exercise forms a major part, the chapter starts with a description of the group of students and the IT component of the course.

Developing IT capability in all Science students

The group of science graduates preparing to teach 'Balanced Science' consists of three subgroups each of which has some opportunity to specialise in one of the sciences, and it is one of these, the 'Science: Physics' group, which features most strongly in this chapter. The Science: Physics students initially possessed a range of knowledge, skills and confidence in IT which ranged from one who had worked for one year managing the computer system in a school, and some who had their own computers, to others who had little expertise in computing and one who not only lacked expertise, but was antipathetic to computing. The Science: Chemistry and Science: Biology groups had generally similar ranges of expertise, although fewer had high level skills, and more had lower level skills.

All PGCE students in the School of Education are given a short IT course aimed at providing an introduction to the general IT facilities in the School and at developing general IT skills in wordprocessing, spreadsheets and databases, but is not related to the use of IT in the students' subjects. A self-profiling system is used to encourage students to identify their IT needs, and then either reinforce their basic skills or extend them via optional sessions. The computers which are used are one of the two kinds which are most commonly used in schools.

The work in science is intended to complement and extend this basic foundation. Most of the computers which are used in science are of the other kind frequently used in schools, in part so that science students have experience of both common systems. Providing an introduction to these computers, without simply repeating the introduction to the School's IT facilities, is achieved by giving the students experience of:
(a) some simple examples of datalogging (using computers with experiments to collect data over time);
(b) a Desk Top Publishing package, in the context of producing work-sheets for science lessons.
The tasks for the latter exercise are differentiated partly to address the range of initial capability and partly to introduce the students to one way of providing differentiation.

In addition to the substantial computing facilities provided in the School and in the science laboratories, the science students also have the opportunity to borrow a palmtop computer for the duration of the course. This gives them opportunities to develop and practise skills in simple wordprocessing, spreadsheets and databases in their own time.

The provision of varied facilities for computing is one part of a general strategy for developing computing capability in all the science students, in which other parts are:

(a) the formal requirement to wordprocess at least one assignment;

(b) the option of completing one or more science assignments which can involve computing;

(c) using clip art and text manipulation software (or at least becoming aware of the existence of such software) to help the production of a display;

(d) providing informal assistance, where possible 'on demand', aimed at solving students' problems and/or taking them a little way on from their current position;

(e) encouraging students to use IT in their teaching;

(f) developing an ethos in which computing is seen to be an important, but also a normal component of science education.

The aim of this part of the course, which is generally done in the first two terms, is that all students should be sufficiently confident with IT in science to use it in their teaching.

Developing IT capability in Science: Physics students

The work done by all science students is extended for the Science: Physics students during the third term in order that they should be sufficiently competent and confident to be able to act as the co-ordinators of IT within the science department in which they will first teach (Tebbutt 1993). This is achieved by further 'training' in datalogging, and the use of spreadsheets in science, but the development of sufficient competence and confidence requires more opportunities for practice than is usually provided in a learning situation.

Thus, it has been the practice for the 'physics' students to set up and run an INSET session on datalogging for the other two groups. This has a number of advantages. The 'physics' students need to match the experiments and activities to the time and number of computers which is available. The information which is given has to have regard to what other groups are doing. Some groups decide to provide worksheets aimed at their colleagues, while others aim their work at pupils, and yet others do something of both. The production of worksheets requires further work in DTP. The physics students' knowledge of datalogging is substantially improved by their own preparation and watching that of others, the inevitable repetition as they demonstrate their experiment to the other groups of students, and taking turns to visit other groups themselves.

Although the INSET session can be quite stressful, the demands on the students are not as great as they would be if they were conducting such sessions away from the immediate support which is provided by fellow students and the tutor. It is the provision of such a 'realistic' situation which is the final stage in the preparation of the students to be IT in science co-ordinators. Since this is a substantial undertaking which needs to be described at some length the whole of the next section is devoted to this.

Developing IT capability via ITT/Consultancy – six Case Studies

The students were placed in schools in pairs, in order to provide some measure of mutual support, and ideally at least one of the pair of students already knew the department as a result of teaching practice, in an attempt to reduce the time and effort needed for familiarisation by both students and department. As tutor, I had worked with each school to identify a suitable problem for the students to tackle. In most cases the need for support in this area was so great that the major difficulty was determining which of the many possible problems were likely to be reasonably soluble by the students with their current state of knowledge, and in the time available for this work.

The nominal time commitment was four half days, but students were aware that more time might be needed than this. The students negotiated their timetables with the schools in order to give them opportunities to monitor progress, and vet potential solutions to their problems and ensure that the final solutions should be as satisfactory as possible. My role in the partnership was to be available to the students on four otherwise non-timetabled occasions in order to provide the help which they might need, and also to visit each school to monitor progress.

The final stage of the project was to devote a fifth half day to a debrief, in which each pair of students described their problem, demonstrated their solution, and described the process by which they reached it. The purpose of this exercise, like all similar ones, was to help the students to evaluate their solution, and to broaden their knowledge by listening to their colleagues' accounts of their activities.

It is now proposed to describe each of the case studies in turn.

School A

Some two years ago this school had been able to buy eight dataloggers (small computers, dedicated to gathering experimental data over time), together with two sensors for use with each datalogger. Its problem was that it had not yet been able to incorporate this equipment into the science curriculum and wished to do so partly because the apparatus represented a considerable financial investment, and partly because the department felt that its use of IT in science needed to be increased. The initial intention was, therefore, to design one or more lessons which involved datalogging and could fit into the department's scheme for Year 8 or Year 9.

As soon as the students started work other problems became apparent.
1. Although both sensors were capable of measuring potentially useful quantities, the range of temperature which the temperature sensor could safely measure was small, and critically, fell substantially short of the boiling point of water.
2. Even though there were enough dataloggers for pupils to collect data in small groups, the department only possessed one of the computers which are needed for processing the data, hence causing a bottleneck in the management of the lesson.

The first problem proved to be very difficult to deal with. Neither the students nor I could think of experiments which would be suitable for Year 8 or 9 pupils and which could be done by utilising the available sensors.

In principle a potential solution to the second problem was that the computer laboratory, housing a substantial number of appropriate computers, was geographically part of the science department, and arrangements might be made to use this facility when datalogging was being done in science lessons. Unfortunately it appeared that these computers needed extra parts before they could be used with the dataloggers.

At this point it was necessary to negotiate a rapid change of plan with the school. It was agreed that the students should continue to familiarise themselves with the datalogger, and to investigate which experiments might be performed if further sensors were purchased. They should then produce a report for the department which would quantify expenditure on sensors and modifications to the computers and indicate to what extent datalogging might then be introduced into the school's curriculum. They should also take some steps to help the science staff to become familiar with the datalogger.

Outcomes

The students handled this change of emphasis well and met the formal requirement to produce a report for the department without difficulty. They were also able to conduct an INSET session on the basic use of the datalogger during a training day whose timing was fortuitous. They have become confident users of the datalogger, and are much more familiar with the potential of datalogging than they were initially. They have developed expertise in recognising the curricular potential of the technique; and in making arguments for different possible development paths, which they have had to cost.

The department can now commit a relatively small amount of further expenditure to purchasing additional sensors. It knows how datalogging can be incorporated in its curriculum, and the staff have some knowledge of the use of the equipment. The change of plan has meant, unfortunately, that the detailed planning of the lessons, complete with the preparation of worksheets for the pupils and guidance sheets for the staff has not been completed.

School B

About three years ago, this science department had purchased six computers which had been mounted on trolleys, in order that computing might be conducted in a variety of ways. For instance single machines might be used in six laboratories at any one time; two machines in each of three laboratories; six machines in a single laboratory; or any combination of these. In addition, the department had bought two examples of about six different sensors, together with six of the devices, called interfaces, which are necessary in order to connect the sensors to the computers. Although the computers had been used since they were purchased, the datalogging equipment had not generally been used – in fact some of the sensors were still sealed in their original packing! Unsurprisingly this department had chosen a problem similar to that of school A, and they wished to have one or more lessons developed which could introduce datalogging in the Year 9 curriculum.

The decisions the students had to take in order to solve the problem were initially logistical, and subsequently curricular. The limited numbers of any one sensor prevented all the pupils tackling one experimental situation at the same time, so the lesson(s) had to be organised as a circus in which pupils circulate round a number (in this case six) different activities. Each of the activities needed to provide an introduction to datalogging but be within the capabilities of the pupils, and be capable of completion within a similar time in order to allow all groups to change activities at once. The students produced a worksheet for each of the stations, having tried the experimental work. A teachers' guide to each experiment, and to the software which was being used, was also necessary because most of the science department staff were unfamiliar with datalogging itself; with the powerful, but unusual software being used; and predictably also with the activities which the students had designed.

Outcomes

The students had gained considerable expertise in the use of the computer–interface–sensor system in use here, and had also improved their general knowledge of datalogging. They had had experience of matching datalogging activities to the curriculum. The production of the worksheets involved them in practising or developing a number of skills. The initial design was subject to evaluation by themselves and others, leading to redesign, all of which involved them in gaining increasing familiarity with a desk top publishing system. The diagrams on the worksheets were produced using a drawing package on the computer, also utilising some examples taken from a library of suitable images held on a CD–ROM.

The school had two lessons which were fully resourced as far as both pupils and teachers were concerned. It was hoped that these lessons would provide the basis for developing expertise in IT among the staff.

School C

This was a large school which had been sufficiently committed to IT in science to arrange that one of the science laboratories should be equipped with eleven computers, connected together in a network so that the same software was easily downloaded on each machine. In spite of this commitment, the use of IT in the science department was both low in quantity and patchy in coverage. The school articulated this problem as the need for curricular materials in either datalogging or the use of spreadsheets in science. Since, coincidentally, support was available from the LEA for datalogging, the students were asked to focus on the use of spreadsheets.

Partly on the basis of a curriculum audit of the science programme for Key Stage 3 and partly on the experience of one of the students trying to teach the topic on teaching practice, the pair decided to construct a spreadsheet exercise around the topic of food. Potentially this is an excellent topic for this technique since it can involve many calculations of quantities such as the contribution of different foodstuffs to the body's need for energy, via carbohydrate or fat; protein; vitamins and fibre. The danger is that the exercise could rapidly become too complex for either pupils or staff, given that neither group was currently familiar with the use of spreadsheets.

The students were already familiar with the idea of using a 'template' – a spreadsheet which has been partially completed and contains the basic framework, data and formulae, or a selection of these depending on the desired demand of the task. They designed such a simple template which was to be used with a worksheet which initially introduced the pupils to the idea of a standard 'portion' of food, listed in the template for a small number of foods, and required them to practise calculating the energy 'content' of 1, 2 or 3 portions of different foods, hence introducing the pupils to the basic technique of entering data into a spreadsheet. The activity progressed by requiring the pupils to weigh one of their number, allowing the spreadsheet to calculate the daily energy requirements of that individual. The pupils determine how much of these energy needs would be provided by a specific lunch. The pupils were then encouraged to make up the energy deficit by simply drinking cooking oil – guessing a quantity for the cooking oil, trying it, and then making subsequent guesses to get as close as possible to the desired figure. Apart from having a certain lugubrious fascination, this task began to use the power of spreadsheets. A third template provided targets for a balanced diet for pupils of a given mass. The pupils were asked to determine how much cooking oil would be required to meet the pupil's daily energy needs, discuss the desirability of such a diet, and finally construct a balanced diet.

Outcomes

The school obtained a complete activity which provided a motivating introduction both to the topic of energy from food, and to the use of spreadsheets. The students had experience of designing and producing the resources which were required. This involved them in learning and becoming proficient with the spreadsheet package in use in the school; analysing the learning material in the course book; designing the activity to provide at least the same learning opportunities as the written material; researching the data needed for the spreadsheet template; and finally designing and producing the worksheets.

School D

Hitherto the teaching of kinetics in this school's science department had been accomplished using wooden trolleys to which was attached narrow, self-adhesive tape, called ticker tape, marked by means of carbon paper and a vibrating arm. The department wished to change this approach, because the technology is rather old, and the data is difficult to interpret. A more modern approach uses light gates to make timings. Originally these were difficult and expensive to use with class experiments. Recently small, dedicated computers have become available which are relatively cheap, and are designed to be very easy indeed to use. The department had decided to use funds derived from placement of students to buy a class set of these devices with their associated light gates and small trolleys which they would otherwise not have been able to afford.

The problem which the students were presented with was to totally redesign the approach to teaching kinetics around the new apparatus, and to produce the appropriate teaching materials. This required them to learn how to use the 'computer'; sort out a teaching approach for a topic which has high conceptual content; consider the modifications which may be necessary for less capable pupils; and finally to design and produce the worksheets which are needed to guide the pupils through the work.

Outcomes

Each aspect of this work provided a challenge for the students. They were initially quite unfamiliar with the dedicated 'computer', and they had had little experience of *designing* an approach to developing concepts as opposed to *teaching* such an approach which had been designed by someone else. As it happens, these students were initially less adept at the use of the DTP package and had to make very considerable progress with this, and with the associated drawing packages. They also made good attempts to achieve differentiation.

Once again, the school benefited from an almost completely developed package of work. They were delighted by the worksheets, not least because they were given the DTP files for them, in order that modifications may easily be made when the package has been used with the pupils.

School E

There was a considerable commitment to IT in this school as a whole, and in the science department. Perhaps for this reason the chosen problem focused on one of the more unusual aspects of IT in science, the use of hypermedia.

A typical hypermedia application might be thought of as a database, providing information about a topic via a number of screens of information, which may be in the form of text, pictures, sounds, or increasingly as video clips. Pupils who are using the application can choose their own path through the data by 'clicking' the mouse on whichever feature they would like to know more about. Clearly, the application designer has to ensure that all the items of information are present, and linked to the 'trigger' which will cause them to be displayed. Since hypermedia applications can, in principle, have many layers of information with a complex pattern of linkages they need some care in construction, and also in use, since it is easy for pupils to get lost.

The department already possessed a hypermedia package which provided information on the Solar System. The task for the students was to develop the application, and to design worksheets which would guide pupils in its use, and spreadsheets which would provide a focus for the data derived from the package.

The students had to become familiar with special software which is available to help the construction process, and enter the data. The arrangement of each screen required many decisions to be made about 'boxes' in which the data was placed such as the number and arrangement of boxes on the screen; the size of each 'box'; the size and font of the text; the colour of the box; and the size, style and content of any pictures. Decisions also had to be made about the links which are to be made between different screens, and what activated these links. Maintaining the flexibility of use of the final product also required the users to be able to return to the beginning whenever they wished to.

In order to encourage the pupils to use the application flexibly, but to some purpose, worksheets were designed which guided the pupils to gather data which was entered into spreadsheets, which were then used to identify patterns either by inspecting the data or by plotting graphs. By this means pupils would be able, for instance, to describe the general variation in the temperature of the planets and deviations from the pattern; they would improve their understanding of the terms 'day' and 'year'; and gain some understanding of what the planets are made of.

Outcomes

The students had to become familiar with the software used to develop the package, with spreadsheets, and with desk top publishing packages for producing the worksheets. They had experience of taking the decisions listed above in designing the application; and in taking the range of decisions which are involved in designing the worksheets and spreadsheets which comprise the rest of the teaching materials.

The department obtained an updated, and much more attractive hyper-media package, together with worksheets which incorporated spread-sheets, as required. Although the teaching materials were substantially complete, further work was still needed to 'polish' the materials, and to provide teachers' notes to guide the use of the package in practice.

School F

The current provision for IT in the science department in this school was low, but the department was anxious to increase this. Since they were receiving support from the LEA for datalogging and spreadsheets in connection with the GEST scheme, this department, like the one above also focused on the provision of hypermedia materials. Unlike school E, however, there were no initial materials for the students to work with, nor any specification for the content to be covered except that it should be derived from the school's Year 9 science course. The students were faced with the difficult task of deciding on the topic when, like all the students, they were as yet unfamiliar with hypermedia. In the event, they chose to concentrate on the animal kingdom.

The parameters of the task are similar to those described above for school E. The hypermedia package which was produced consisted of forty-six screens containing text, pictures and sounds, which were linked in a complex fashion which allowed a variety of ways of interrogating the materials.

Outcomes

As at school E, the students had to become familiar with the software used to develop the application, and to practise using desk top publishing packages for producing the worksheets. They had experience of taking a range of decisions in designing the application (similar to those listed above); and in designing the worksheets which comprise the rest of the teaching materials.

The department obtained a complete hypermedia stack which was matched in content and language with the course books being used in the department. The worksheets which were produced to guide the pupils' work with the application were differentiated to cater for a range of abilities.

Evaluation of the Project

Each of the schools benefited from the project by receiving materials which they would otherwise not have possessed, usually at the expense of a very small amount of staff input. Most of the packages were substantially complete, but few were absolutely finished, and they would, in any case, be likely to benefit from the advice of experienced members of staff.

Every group of students had excellent opportunities to practise their existing skills, both in computing and in developing teaching materials, and many were able to develop new ones. The most notable benefit was the students' gain in confidence. This was such that most of them could be expected to have the expertise and confidence to act as the IT in science co-ordinator in their schools from the time they take up their appointment.

As tutor I had the benefit of testing whether ideas could be successfully implemented at all, particularly in the challenging context of solving problems identified by the schools, and in the hands of students with relatively limited experience of both teaching and IT.

Although this was the first time that this exercise had been carried out, it seemed to have such substantial benefits for each of the components of the partnership that it provides the basis for similar projects in the future. Perhaps the most telling comment is that a school which could not be accommodated in this first trial has already booked its place in the next one.

CHAPTER 6

Mathematics partnership

This chapter describes an activity set up during the PGCE mathematics course which involved two tutors in the university, mentors in twenty schools in the West Midlands, forty PGCE students and a large number of pupils. We think that learning about teaching is an ongoing process and ideas are best redeveloped when we challenge our practice in discussion with colleagues. The assessment and moderation activity described below offered opportunities for discussion in college and schools with the students being the intermediaries, allowing ideas to be worked on over a period of time.

As tutors, our role was similar to that of the ancient encyclopaedists gathering data from many lands. Whilst the National Curriculum offers a common content base, the practices and philosophies of teaching and assessment are very different in schools, with each mathematics department making decisions in relation to their particular needs, circumstances and available resources. Consequently for each curriculum decision that has to be made (setting or mixed ability, textbook or practical work, simultaneous equation before trigonometry) there are many 'right' solutions. A school offers a particular orthodoxy: forty students working in twenty schools gives us the data to help the students recognise particular orthodoxies and allow them to be shared, challenged and explained.

We planned the structure of the 1993–94 PGCE course with a group of teachers during the Easter of the preceding academic year and produced a programme for the year. One of the issues during these discussions was how to use the times when students return to the university during a school placement (see Figure 6.1, stage 3 and stage 5). It was our practice in previous years to use these sessions for students to share concerns, to do some mathematics or to deal with an issue which was immediately relevant to what was happening in a particular student's classroom. The group of teachers thought that we should use these times to include ways of working with the students that would enhance the practice in schools and at the university as well as making the links between schools and university stronger.

At our first mentor meeting early in September we discussed the programme for the year and raised the issue about the time during the first school placement when the students return to the university. In the November of the Autumn term, pairs of students are in schools for a three week school experience but return to the university on each Friday afternoon for a three hour session. Could we link the work in the university, with the work in school to the advantage of all involved? Many ideas were floated. One was the different examination syllabuses followed by schools, another the different texts used. The mentors said that they would find it useful to know who was using the same examination boards or same textbooks in order to link and improve their own practice through considering the ways in which other departments are working. By returning to the university with the different practices from the schools, the students would recognise the diversity among the departments and we could organise discussion to try to account for the choices made. Additionally we could provide through the students feedback to the schools of the practices of other schools in the area.

This model of the students acting as gatherers and providers of information as well as learners was thought to be a good idea. Eventually we decided to work on the role and practice of Ma1, (the first attainment target in the Mathematics National Curriculum, described as Using and Applying Mathematics, relating to process rather than content). During the discussion with mentors, it became clear that this attainment target was an area of concern for schools. It was certainly an area that we needed to explore carefully with the students as, in the format presented in the National Curriculum, it would be outside their own school experience. The mentors were interested to know how other schools worked on this particular attainment target with their pupils, raising issues such as:

– Was there a particular format to lessons involving Ma1?
– How often was Ma1 considered to be part of mathematics lessons?
– How was it to be assessed and how often?
– What was recorded?
– Were the words used to describe the levels in Ma1 interpreted similarly across departments?
– What level were the pupils attaining?
– What was said to the pupils about this particular attainment target?
– How did schools relate this attainment target to coursework in GCSE?
– What practices were being used for moderation and validation of the NC levels?

During the Autumn term we worked on Ma1 with the students, by looking at activities, analysing the mathematics and offering our own interpretation of this very important attainment target. In previous years students would have been expected to work on Ma1 within the schools, but by formalising the link between university and school work, mentors felt that the differing ideas would be more carefully considered and contrasted. The discussion and observation of what was offered in different schools would allow students to obtain a wider picture of varied practices.

It was decided that the students would set an open task for pupils during this first teaching practice. They would mark the work and formally assess for Ma1, using the statements within the levels, with the help of the mentors. This was felt to be a good way of creating an opportunity for discussion in school about Ma1 as the mentors and other members of the department would offer advice on the planning of the activity. By bringing the work into the university for moderation, students would be able to discuss perceptions of what constituted evidence for Ma1, and would be able to disseminate the ideas back in school.

The process began to take on the form shown in Figure 6.1.

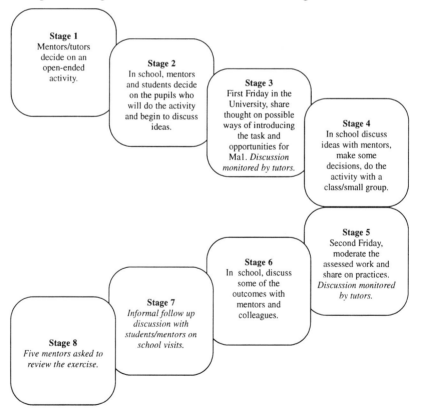

Figure 6.1

This was an opportunity to consider the coming together of theory and practice in the teaching and learning of mathematics with reference to Ma1 through the students working on an activity with the pupils in different schools. The student has to adapt the generalised statements about a theoretical framework for Ma1 to the particular circumstances of the school situation. Hopefully we would all learn from the many decisions about practice.

What we were also interested in discovering from the exercise were:
- Was the exercise useful in helping the students bridge the theory–practice divide?
- Does asking all students to work on the same task offer a good discussion base for sessions in the university?
- Does a common task enable points of discussion to move from the university out to the schools?
- Does the sharing of ideas from other schools offer a practical gain to schools?

Stage 1: The Activity

The activity itself could have been chosen from a wide selection. The mentor group decided it was important that the task should be as open-ended as possible so that many decisions would have to be taken by the students leading the lesson. These decisions would include, for example:
- the starting description;
- the grouping of pupils;
- the time allowed;
- the number of choices that would be offered to the pupils.

Many of these decisions would have to be made in relation to the particular school contexts – departmental policies, classroom practices, age and experiences of the pupils and resources. Given the short time available it was decided to use a task which had been sent to the students to work on during the summer before the course began[1]. This meant that all the students would have had the opportunity to work on the problem at their own level, would have already engaged in some analysis of the mathematics and some reflection on their own learning. We hoped that as a consequence the students would be ready to discuss implications for the teaching and learning of this particular task for the pupils.

The task chosen, Figure 6.2, comes from *Hole Numbers* (Bell *et al.* 1992, p.39).

---

[1] Working on open-ended tasks, one of the aims of Ma1, would be new to many of our students despite most of them having achieved a degree in mathematics. Our time with them in the Autumn term is relatively short and there are many areas to cover. We decided to offer some experience of working on open-ended and investigational activities prior to starting the course and sent them several mathematical problems to work on in the summer holiday. During the Autumn term we asked the students to bring their solutions so that as a group we could spend time on analysis and reflection of such work.

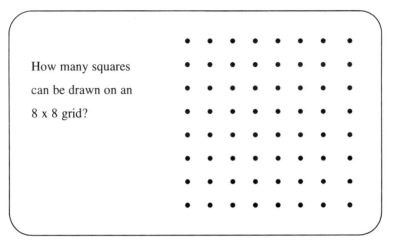

How many squares
can be drawn on an
8 x 8 grid?

Figure 6.2

Stage 2: Planning for the Task

During the first week in school the students decided with their mentors, which classes or groups of children would work on the problem. This varied from school to school. Some students worked with Year 7, others with Years 8 and 9. One student worked with a small group of Year 10, extracting the group from a lesson taught by the class teacher. Decisions were affected by such things as:

  – which classes the student was timetabled to teach;
  – the class where two students were team teaching;
  – the behaviour of pupils;
  – the experience of pupils in working with open tasks.

Only in one school did the activity appear inappropriate, as the task chosen was one used for an end of year assessment. The problem was resolved by the students in this school working with a small group who had met the problem before.

Stage 3: Making Decisions

The students reported on some of the practical decisions made in school during their return on the first Friday. They came to this meeting with information on their placement schools' current practice and understanding of Ma1. In small groups these different practices were shared. The teaching approaches for Ma1 varied. One major difference lay in the amount of structure they offered to pupils. Expectations were also different. For example some teachers, beforehand, felt that the problem was an easy one for Year 7 whilst others thought that it was testing for Year 9. These judgements were not always related to the achievement of the pupils. The discussion revealed to the students the varied reactions and approaches amongst teachers and reinforced once more the idea that there is no 'right' way.

Having considered the school based decisions, we moved to more detailed discussion of the lessons themselves. We had already had sessions on Ma1 (based on NCC (1992)) which had focused on opportunities for pupil choice. We then shared ideas about possible settings and structures for the problem, and lesson plans were outlined by the students. It was interesting to hear the range of ideas from the schools and we added a few of our own.

The decisions about the task made by the students involved:

The format
  – structured worksheet guiding throughout the task
  – a step by step approach, two by two grid, three by three, etc
  – a printed copy of the original task
  – demonstration on the board showing some squares

Recording
  – prepared table to fill in answers
  – free choice

Resources
  – square paper
  – geo-boards

The style of the work
  – independently
  – co-operatively, pairs, small groups

The presentation of the work
  – individual
  – group

Any likely sources of difficulty
  – possible misconceptions
  – language of presentation

The discussion at this stage focused on the richness of possibilities available, whilst one of the areas of possible error that many students considered is shown in Figure 6.3.

being accepted
as a square

but this shape is a
'diamond', not a square

Figure 6.3

When they returned to school their lesson plans were formalised. Some of the schools allowed the students to plan in relation to the students' own understanding of the problem and interpretations of Ma1. Other schools offered more directed advice, in line with their own policy. But all were generous in the help offered with the lesson planning. Mentors commented that they enjoyed hearing the different ideas which had been generated in the student groups.

Stage 4: In the Classroom

The activity was carried out in schools. The students appreciated the help they felt they had received from the discussion of the task with others. For some it gave them the confidence to be adaptable when misunderstandings arose, for others it offered questions to ask or ways of introducing extension ideas. Some of the mentors who observed/joined in with the activity talked of learning a lot from the responses of their pupils to the questions. Some also felt that by helping the students to plan, hearing about possible choices and observing the actual lesson, they gained a different perspective on the tasks and on their own teaching.

In discussion with the class teachers, the students marked and assessed the pupils' work, identifying aspects of Ma1 with reference to the National Curriculum statements.

Stage 5: Moderation

On the second Friday, the students returned with samples of the assessed work where they considered there was evidence to support particular Statements of Attainment in Ma1. In groups the students moderated the work across the schools, (students from the same school worked in different groups). Pupils' responses varied across the ten levels. In some cases students were easily able to agree the assignment of a level to a piece of work, while for other work there was much argument. As well as comparing the written evidence in front of them, the students needed time to compare the pupils' responses during the lessons. This highlighted the need for evidence in different forms and how you need to offer such evidence in a moderation exercise. For those working in schools with large groups of pupils who are emergent bilinguals, they reported that they saw and heard much mathematics being done, but there was little or no writing to support this. For some students the lack of writing was no bar to them giving high levels to the pupils as they had annotated the pupils' work with observations and quotations. Although the work had been assessed by the students, some of the schools valued it sufficiently to want the pupils' work returned to be put into their coursework files. This was a bonus for many of the students and made them feel that they were equal partners in the process.

An additional outcome of this moderation activity was the opportunity to discuss progression within Ma1. Defining such progression is often elusive because of the nature of this attainment target. For example, what does hypothesising look like at the ages of seven, eleven and fourteen? The activity was carried out with pupils across a range of ages and achievement. The evidence from the different levels offered a practical basis for students to analyse the meaning of statements of attainment and what they understood by progression.

Stage 6: Report Back

Most of the students felt that they had gained from the exercise and in particular wanted to report back on discussions of individual's work to teachers in their schools, especially on a comparative level. The report back to schools tended to be on an informal basis probably as we had created no structure for this with mentors or students, nor offered pointers to the students of what might be particularly useful.

Stages 7 and 8: In Retrospect

From discussion with the students and mentors, it was clear that the exercise was valued, but there were some reservations, especially in ways in which the dissemination to schools could be made even more useful.

One issue for the students was the task itself. It was felt that it was not necessarily the best choice for the assessment and moderation exercise. Although most students stated that they and the pupils had gained from the work and enjoyed it, the task did not explicitly demand a great deal of explanation and justification, one of the strands of Ma1. It was sufficient in many cases for pupils to draw diagrams and it was clear what decisions had been made without them writing much. Perhaps a task which requires explanation of decision making might offer more practice in assessing writing and offer a basis for even more interesting discussion about Ma1.

The time for the activity was very limited, especially the moderation. The assessment had had to be done in a very few days, or even overnight and the students would have liked more opportunity to reflect on the assessment and discuss it further with their mentors before trying a moderation exercise. One suggestion was that a shorter task might be the answer, for this time period, with the whole process repeated during the Spring term teaching practice. Certainly many of the mentors and students felt that the process was of such value it was worth repeating.

The feedback by the students to schools about the moderation task was limited, as so early in the course the students were unable to generalise the discussions they had shared with particular students. One of the mentors

suggested that a pre-course meeting of mentors might draw up a sheet of questions related to the task chosen and the lesson style to help students focus on areas which would be of wide interest. As the feedback was informal, general guidelines for students' collection of data were offered as being useful points of dissemination:
- starting points, how the tasks are to be introduced;
- age/achievement of pupils;
- lesson style;
- evidence to support a particular statement of attainment.

It was also suggested that a departmental meeting might be set aside to allow students a more formal setting for dissemination, spreading ideas more effectively, and allowing for a lead in to practical discussions of Ma1.

When other mentors were asked about using such meetings, many endorsed the idea, especially those who stated that the exercise was so valuable it should be repeated with a different activity during the Spring term. The students might be able to report on the moderation stage in a more formal way which would offer the school a more tangible basis for departmental discussion. Copies of pupils' work might help to disseminate ideas further, a portfolio of evidence for particular statements of attainment could be produced. The students' ability to recognise evidence for Ma1 might be improved, so selections of pupils' work across schools would perhaps be more pertinent.

One of the areas of mismatch in Ma1 was over the lesson style. There were mentors who wished to see an open style of presentation (with the pupils having to make decisions as to which questions to ask and answer) who saw students offering structured worksheets. Similarly there were mentors who expected students to offer structured worksheets who observed students using a more open style. This indicated to us how much more carefully we need to share our ideas about Ma1 with students and mentors, and how much more we need to find out about schools' work. In our first meeting with mentors we concentrated on how we worked on lesson planning with students, and whilst this needs to be expanded, it may be that we need to consider this in relation to lesson styles for Ma1.

What have we gained?

Was the exercise useful in helping the students bridge the theory–practice divide? We doubt that the students would express it in those terms, but they certainly appreciated the three way input from other students, their mentors and class teachers and their tutors.

Does asking all students to work on the same task offer a good discussion base for sessions in the university? From watching our forty students work on the issue, we can report success; certainly individuals reflected on the level of the discussion, and we enjoyed joining in with many aspects. Having work from twenty schools certainly offered useful material for such sessions.

Does a common task enable points of discussion to move from the university out to the schools? This is more problematic. There was evidence of aspects of the students' discussions moving out into schools, and some individuals felt that their schools gained more than others did. The formalisation of the dissemination may help with this in a future exercise.

Does the sharing of ideas from other schools offer a practical gain to schools? This seemed very limited, but perhaps as more material is collected, pupils' work might become the medium for such transfers.

The exercise was certainly of great value to the students and it provided a valuable exercise related to their future practice in a way which could not be achieved by their working solely in schools or solely in the university. The opportunity to discuss the activity with mentors, both before and after the task, and to have all our twenty plus schools working on the same idea offers an excellent example of the advantages of partnership.

CHAPTER 7

Partnership in Modern Foreign Languages: Intensive Language Sessions

Introduction

The term 'intensive' is subject to a variety of interpretations in the literature, but predominantly it refers to a spell of foreign language teaching with a more extended programme of activities than normal, to courses abroad or to 'sections bilingues' (see, for example, Hawkins 1988). The three intensive sessions reported here were concerned not with teaching or practising the foreign language but with the productive use of it, and all conformed to a broadly similar format whereby pupils of a certain year group spent a period of time outside the context of normal lessons completing a series of communicative tasks, hearing and speaking only the foreign language. The Summer term was thought to be particularly suitable for these sessions because it seemed a useful way of rekindling pupils' interest after their examinations. Moreover, students had also finished their teaching practice and consequently had better expertise with learners than earlier in the course, and were in a position to accept the challenge.

The whole programme was, like the PGCE course itself, posited on a partnership bond, in which each partner was invaluable to the other. In her discussion of a partnership framework Stone (1993) wrote that 'individual partnerships and courses should...be based on a principle of shared ownership and responsibility' (p.18), but goes on to point out that 'clearly there are certain very specific contributions which can only be made by one particular partner' (p.20). The importance of the HEI lay firstly in the catalytic role played by the tutor in negotiating with the mentor and co-ordinating the trainees' input with the teachers' knowledge of the pupils' capabilities; and secondly in the tutor's subject expertise which enabled students to understand the methodological principles of the event and relate them to other aspects of the course as well as to the relevant literature.

Aims and rationale

There were a variety of aims in putting on these sessions. Firstly, it seemed a splendid opportunity to benefit from the existing partnership scheme by jointly planning and executing a part of the curriculum for a given age group: teacher trainees could be tapped to provide the large number of foreign language speakers required at no extra cost to the school and the teacher could suggest the types of task suitable for the chosen pupils. Secondly, it was thought that such a venture would help to cement mutual understanding in approaches to problems of methodology in teaching and learning foreign languages. Thirdly, and undoubtedly the most important aim in terms of foreign language methodology, this type of session seemed tailor-made for giving pupils direct access to a situation in which they could indulge in the freer and more productive use of the foreign language, as distinct from the type of practice to which normal classroom work often confines them. With some variation depending on age, ability and attainment level, learning stages in the methodology of foreign language teaching follow the broad pattern of introduction, practice, reproduction, production and freer use, in which the tasks set become more genuinely communicative in type as the learner progresses from practice to use.

The fourth aim, closely tied to the third, was to help pupils realise, indeed feel the communicative value of the language they were learning to use and to observe at first hand the impact they made on others when they spoke it. As all teachers of modern languages know only too well, one of the most difficult tasks they have is to motivate pupils to learn. The fifth aim therefore was to view these sessions as a source of motivation, which meant that the tasks set had to be guaranteed to afford a major degree of success, needed to be as lifelike as possible and be presented as fun to carry out. Sixthly, arising from the idea of real life language tasks, it was considered valuable to foster pupils' independence in the use of the foreign language: the situation seemed ideal for encouraging learners to rely on their own resourcefulness, by trying out a variety of communicative strategies should language problems arise. Finally, considering the length of time involved, these sessions were viewed as excellent for offering relatively lengthy exposure to the foreign language – a vital component in successful acquisition, well documented in the literature. They could provide a spell of time in which only the foreign language was continuously heard – a type of short 'immersion' period.

Organisation

Three groups of trainees undertook intensive language activities in two schools. Two of the groups ran German and French activities for Year 9 pupils parallel in the same school on the same morning, and are identified as groups 1a and 1b; the third group, group 2, organised French activities in a different school for Year 8 pupils.

A feature of organisation common to all was the visit of the respective Heads of Department to the School of Education, after consultation with the university tutors, to outline the nature and size of pupil groups, the logistical structure of the day including timings and available space, and the range of topics covered by the target pupils. Emphasis in all cases was placed on the fact that pupils were not to be taught, rather to be given the opportunity to use what language they had already learnt in a genuinely communicative setting. Owing to the nature of topics covered by the pupils a town scene was suggested in each case to provide them with the opportunity of visiting a variety of shops and services, where all realia used were authentic.

There were, however, differences in emphasis between groups 1 and 2. The school working with group 2 had negotiated with the students and produced a booklet for pupils to complete as they proceeded from one activity to the next, so that to a large extent the content, particularly in terms of linguistic structure, was defined. This was seen as desirable in order to avoid the possibility of too great a mismatch between trainee expectations and pupil capabilities. Group 1, working with older pupils, had a much freer rein and were encouraged to experiment. The potential problem of mismatch was avoided by a visit of the trainee team leaders with their tutor to the school a few days before the event to check linguistic content and discuss possible problems with the relevant class teachers. This also gave them the opportunity to loan props available in the department. Attention was also drawn in all three groups to particular pupils who might need special handling because of behaviour difficulties or reticence.

Groups 1a and 1b were to take over rooms and corridors in the languages teaching area, since the main school halls were being used for GCSE examinations. Group 2 had the luxury of a separate fifth form centre with an attached sandwich bar which could be incorporated into a café scene.

Implementation

Group 1a

Four sets of pupils, totalling 110, engaged in various activities, each for an hour. They were welcomed to the town of Besançon, issued with a quiz sheet containing a few simple questions in the target language about the three locations to be visited, and divided into three subgroups for the period. They were to visit in turn the 'Office de Tourisme', the 'PTT' and the 'Café'.

At the Office de Tourisme, pupils were instructed to find the way to specific places and draw the route on a map, find out about other activities in the town which may interest them, book an advance ticket for the cinema after enquiring about times and prices, and use a listening post to find out more about the town. There was also a 'spot the ball' style competition based on a map of France.

The PTT activity involved buying a 'Carte Jeune' by cheque and the purchase and writing of a postcard. Pupils were interviewed by an employee of the PTT who filled in an application form on their behalf before asking them to verify and sign it, and worksheets were available to provide help with the cheque and the postcard.

A quick revision of food and drink items by means of flashcards preceded the café scene, and led into an information gap activity performed with partners based on the completion of a menu. Pupils were then selected to serve orange juice and biscuits to their peers, with prompt-posters on the walls to help them to initiate and sustain dialogue.

Group 1b

The German group followed a different structure. Here two sets of pupils totalling fifty were involved, each for a two hour session. The German staff had requested that the town session be preceded by a series of warm up activities during the first hour, to revive the necessary vocabulary and structures and give the pupils more confidence.

Pupils were put into subgroups as they entered; the first hour was structured into four sessions with groups moving tables at fifteen minute intervals. One session revised shopping vocabulary by means of a game of snakes and ladders – pupils had to correctly identify the item on a mini flashcard before being allowed to throw the dice. Another worked on directions and places in the town based on a map of Hutstadt, the imaginary town invented by the students. A third dealt with café vocabulary and structures in the form of menus and roleplays, whereas the fourth constituted an explanation of and preparation for the ensuing town visit. Pupils were issued with German cardboard money supplied by the school, and given a passport form to complete. The passport also contained symbols of the six locations to be visited in the town. At each location pupils were to gain the signature of the shopkeeper to say that they had completed the required tasks, and also write down the password; this was to be identified by the shopkeeper's removal of his or her hat and scratching of the head. Once all six boxes had been signed pupils completed crossword puzzles and quizzes based on the event whilst awaiting the issue of a certificate commemorating their visit to Hutstadt.

For the second hour pupils were randomly divided into smaller groups and sent to their first destination, with instructions that they were then free to proceed through the town at their own pace, alone or with friends, accomplishing tasks in whichever order they wished. Locations to be visited were the underground station, information office, café, post office, supermarket and clothes shop. Much use was made throughout of prompt-posters and cue cards to help the less able or the less imaginative.

Group 2

The thirty pupils of French in Group 2 started by playing a series of five different board games, in which some of the language used reinforced that needed later in the shop situations. Some games had posters which prompted possible language they might use. Each group of pupils played each game for about ten minutes. Subsequently, pupils were issued with a booklet containing tasks to be fulfilled in which results could be noted in a minimal amount of writing. As if on a visit to France, they passed through customs where they had to answer details about themselves and then proceeded to the bank to 'change' money – in fact they received a quantity of paper franc notes of different denominations, sufficient to cover purchases in the shops. At the bank they were asked to show the 'passport' they had previously made, answer questions on it and ask about the rate of exchange.

The shops in the town consisted of 'une alimentation', 'un syndicat d'initiative', 'une agence de voyage', 'une pharmacie' and 'une maison de la presse'. The booklets helped to orientate their questioning in the various shops. Examples of tasks were asking for articles, finding out prices (none were visible) and checking their change, asking whether various goods were available or whether the town had certain facilities and where they were, and enquiring about directions and transport to different places and locating them on the map. While going round the town they were also invited to talk to a 'stranger' and to find out his/her personal details. Two types of reward for communication were offered in the form of different coloured stars stuck into the booklet by the students, depending on the amount of success achieved in fulfilling the tasks.

At the end of the morning pupils entered the café where they had to ask for and purchase food and drink and sit down and 'chat' to students at the tables.

Evaluations

Pupil evaluations

Pupil reactions inevitably varied considerably from the outright enthusiast to the critic who describes everything as boring. On the whole, however, comments were very positive and there were some significant similarities in the replies given.

Group 1a

Pupils on the whole found the activities worthwhile. Of the fourteen who said they were not, eleven nevertheless registered some benefit in answer to a later question. Bearing in mind the aims of the session (language use rather than teaching), it was interesting to note a few replies commenting that they 'had not learnt anything new' or that 'we had already done all the work'. At the other extreme were a few pupils who felt the session was not useful because they had understood little of what was being said.

The favourite activity by far was the café, mainly due to the free drink and biscuit, although one individual complained about the quality of the squash! Other reasons given were that it was the easiest to understand and to become involved in. One or two pupils preferred the post office or information office because they were 'more of a challenge' as well as giving a wider range of activities in different skills.

Reasons for not liking an activity were mainly not understanding what to do, because instructions were not clear enough and were spoken too quickly, and the lack of sufficient time to complete the tasks.

Pupils did appreciate the effort involved in setting up such an event, and enjoyed the emphasis on speaking, as well as the practical nature of the activities and the use of French throughout. Several spoke of the more creative role which they were asked to play, the greater involvement and realism and the benefits of working in smaller groups with more 'teachers'.

The majority of pupils were aware of the benefits of going over work which they had done before and putting topics together in what they saw as a major, practical revision exercise enabling them to 'try and test' their skills. Three quarters of the pupils said that they had gained practical knowledge about the way things work in France, and would feel much more confident about coping in a French town. Suggestions for improvement mainly centred upon students speaking more slowly and on allowing more time for each activity. About a quarter of the replies also made a plea for more English to be spoken, although this often clashed with their recognition of the benefits of consistent exposure to French.

Better explanations were called for before the session started.

In summary, almost all pupils had enjoyed the session and found it an entertaining and interesting change from normal classroom activities.

Group 1b

All the German pupils replied that they had found the activities worthwhile, and many of the replies were extremely positive. Several pupils commented on the great amount of effort which had gone into trying to make the day interesting for them.

Pupils found it more difficult to identify a favourite activity. Likes and dislikes were much more evenly spread, and a variety of reasons were given to justify the statements made. No one activity was generally found to be appreciably more difficult than the others.

There was much more consensus on how the session differed from normal lessons. Many spoke of an interesting, refreshing change, and enjoyed the atmosphere of moving around a 'real' German town. The emphasis on oral work was noticed, as was the insistence on speaking and hearing German throughout with a variety of different people. The coverage of many different topics together instead of concentrating on one at a time was another clear feature.

The benefits felt by all pupils were also fairly homogeneous. Most spoke of refreshing their memory on topics they had done before and brushing up their German: 'we were practising and putting our German to use and sometimes without realising it'. Most spoke of increased confidence in using the language, several saying that they found they knew more German than they thought. A common comment was that they felt they would be able to cope now if they visited a German town.

Suggestions for improvements were few. One or two suggested that more time should be devoted to the activities, that the café should have provided real food and drink, and that there should be a prize for the first person with all the correct answers. One pupil suggested the inclusion of harder words which had not been covered before 'so you have to think about the sentence', and another called for 'more learning, as we already knew how to say everything'. This echoed the view of another pupil who said that the German used wasn't very challenging. Most pupils however were impressed by the thoroughness of organisation.

Group 2

Enjoyment was once more a major factor with the event described as a 'fun way of learning'. Here too pupils appreciated the amount of effort which had been put into preparation and were positive in their feedback.

The café was the most popular activity, probably because of the food involved, with the games a close second. Comments were made about the realism of the situations, the feeling of 'going to France', especially when given the opportunity of using French money. The majority of pupils liked most of the activities though one or two comments were made about the queue waiting to go through customs and the need for more variety of activities in the shops. A few commented too on the frustration of all the shopkeepers speaking French and refusing to speak English, a parallel to group 1a, whereas the German group saw this solely as an advantage.

Reactions to the booklet were varied. Most pupils found it helpful to give a sense of orientation, to guide them to collecting information and help them to ask questions, and appreciated the merit system as a way of charting their progress and getting rewards. One or two, however, found it demoralising and unhelpful, and thought that there was too much writing involved.

Confidence was here again recognised as the key benefit. Pupils had found the session easier than they had expected, felt that they would now know what to do when they went to France, and felt competent at handling French money. A few pupils stated that they had learnt new vocabulary and phrases, which highlights the reality of language acquisition in a target language environment even if teaching is not intended, and underlines most strongly the need for maximum use of target language in the classroom.

Student evaluations

Benefits to pupils

Many of the points mentioned under what students saw as benefits accruing to the pupils confirmed fulfilment of a number of the aims of the sessions. These included the sense of fun which they thought pupils experienced despite being thrown in the deep end and asked to survive in different contexts more real for them than ordinary work in class. Several trainees noticed that as pupils were obliged either to use what they had learnt or to resort to their own ingenuity in overcoming language problems a certain degree of self-reliance was being fostered in them to the point where, in some cases, when encountering success in fulfilling a particular communicative task pupils were seen to register genuine surprise at having made themselves understood to a stranger, thereby suddenly realising the force of the foreign language as a means of communication.

Another frequently mentioned point was that the availability of a much larger number of foreign language speakers than was possible in normal class conditions seemed to create a greater sense of awareness of the foreign language in pupils' minds; consequently they appeared less inclined than in class to use their native language as they encountered different members of the foreign language speaking community. Students also commented on the nature of the relationship between pupils as language users and themselves as unknown speakers of the foreign language: pupils regarded them as people rather than teachers. Three particular points were identified in support of this view: firstly, that the students acted as sympathetic native speakers, respecting any recognisably comprehensible attempts at communication; secondly, that there was no correction of the pupils' foreign language allowed in that the message was either understood and the communicative purpose achieved or it was not and negotiation ensued until needs were satisfied; and thirdly, that because the trainees were outsiders, and therefore did not share the teachers' knowledge of their pupils' language content and ability, a genuine opportunity was presented for exploiting the real and unrehearsed use of the foreign language and the information gap which existed, no expectation of particular language items being present.

Finally students indicated that the possibility of differentiated activities was much greater than in class, since activities could be constructed so that more able pupils could have access to more demanding tasks than weaker ones, but that, nevertheless, all could experience the satisfaction of some kind of communicative fulfilment.

Comments on the games and tasks set

Advantages were seen in putting group games at the start of the session. They provided a strong element of fun, which helped to break the ice initially, creating a friendly and undaunting atmosphere for the pupils. Another advantage was that the language used in the games was transferable to some of the tasks which they were then asked to perform, which helped the less confident pupils. Generally it was reported that the pupils found the tasks very enjoyable and highly motivating and although some found a little difficulty in completing them, a few of the better pupils could have been further extended perhaps by more non-transactional types of task.

Effects on training and future thinking

There were a range of positive comments alluding to the chance which these sessions gave learners to indulge in the freer use of language. Many trainees endorsed the view that participation in these sessions had drawn particular attention to the importance of this aspect of language: one student called it 'an area which I have neglected to devote enough time and thought to'. Others wrote of the opportunity afforded them to witness in action the ultimate aim of teaching a foreign language. They were pleased to be in a position to observe the product of foreign language learning rather than the process which normally characterises work in class and to find out about the real oral capability of pupils of a particular background, age and attainment. One student claimed to have become more aware of the way in which different aspects of the methodology course integrated throughout the PGCE year, saying that the intensive language session had 'brought many aspects of the course together'. Several noted that the experience had left them with a clearer view of how to implement communicative practice beyond the scope of classroom procedures, while others reflected on the vital importance of practising language structures in class before communicative competence can be tried out, thus revealing a sharper appreciation of the planning and direction of lesson materials and activities.

Perhaps one of the most interesting points raised was that of working in close co-operation with schools: not only were they working independently of their university tutors in the latter stages, but also involved with teachers at a level of mutual respect rather than as student teachers under the direction of certain school staff. Furthermore, they felt as though they were supplying a need which teachers could not provide and in so doing making their own contribution to the pupils' education.

Teacher evaluations

Teacher reaction was also very positive. They felt that pupils had enjoyed the sessions, used their language in authentic situations and had the chance to observe interaction in the target language between outsiders as well as to engage in conversation with them, thus broadening their total language experience. This was a bonus which was difficult for the school staff to provide. Pupils had been helped to consolidate their work, and to view classwork as useful as well as seeing the links between different topics rather than experiencing them in isolation over a spread of lessons. Staff had the opportunity to observe pupils working with others who were unknown to them; it was interesting for them to note to what extent their pupils regarded the use of the foreign language as a reality.

The opening activities employed in groups 1b and 2 were seen as creating a safe environment in which to practise the vocabulary before moving on to explore the town, as well as providing a better opportunity for explaining instructions more carefully. More time was clearly needed to avoid the rush experienced by group 1a and to allow pupils to feel their way into the activities.

The whole event was seen as a very motivating and worthwhile experience for both pupils and staff; one teacher reported that it had encouraged pupils to want to go on a trip abroad. All staff seemed quite keen to repeat the venture in future years and indeed mentors from other schools have since expressed a desire to be involved in similar sessions.

Conclusions

It is clear that partnership between the schools and the HEI provided an ideal basis for a complementary contribution from each side to the pupils' education in modern foreign languages. Schools were given access to a wide range of ideas, support and resources generated by the HEI and tailored to the specific needs they defined. These joint ventures also illuminated two facets of proper language use: not only did pupils have the opportunity to try out their communicative strategies working with a known number of language items practised by the school, but as the tasks were set by outsiders not so familiar with the pupils' knowledge, a degree of unpredictability – at the heart of all real dialogue – was introduced into the communicative exchanges. Close collaboration on one hand was offset by an element of the unknown on the other.

In terms of outcomes the evaluations amply confirmed fulfilment of the original aims and revealed that all participants found the experience not only educationally fruitful but also very enjoyable. At an organisational level the chief suggestions for improvement were that the time allowed should be no shorter than two hours to allow for familiarisation, movement and participation and that pupils should be informed more clearly beforehand that using the language rather than learning it was the main objective. Being normally used to progressive presentation and practice of new language in class, some pupils thought that they had not learnt enough! At the level of ideas and activities the experience sparked off many suggestions limited only by the imagination of the organisers. It also alerted students and teachers to the importance of not neglecting the final productive stage in foreign language learning, to the extent that the students felt inspired to organise similar collaborative projects in their future schools.

CHAPTER 8

Partnership in Physical Education

Introduction

During the early stages of any PGCE course, students need to acquire confidence in working with children and to translate into practice the content of their university-based teaching. Consequently the physical education course has always included a significant component of school-based work, over and above that of teaching practice.

Originally, when numbers of students were small (12) it was relatively easy to take the whole group into one school to carry out some games-based work with a single class of pupils. It was felt that the combination of relatively small groups of children and an area of the curriculum with which most students felt comfortable was conducive to a positive introduction to teaching in school. In this positive climate it was also possible for students to begin to develop basic teaching skills.

Within a very short time the activity emphasis shifted to gymnastics in order to improve students' subject knowledge in this area while continuing to focus on the confidence and the teaching skills which had featured in the earlier games-based work. Supplementing the university-based work in gymnastics with the work with pupils proved to be very successful. It also ensured, at a time when opportunities to teach this activity were very limited in some schools and when approaches to its teaching were very varied, that students had a common experience of one approach to teaching which fostered high levels of achievement for pupils of varied abilities including some whose performance level was high.

At a later stage, dance was added as another activity area for this development and extension work. At the time, it was proving difficult to ensure that all female students had experience of teaching dance during teaching practice and next to impossible to obtain any kind of dance teaching experience for male students. For the students this school-based experience, supplementing the dance course during the early stages of the

PGCE year, provided much needed confidence and a sense of achievement in an activity area where few had much previous experience.

In addition to the gymnastics and dance work undertaken, the swimming aspect of the course had always incorporated work with pupils. Initially, schools using the university pool had been offered assistance from the student group who had learned to plan lessons and to teach small groups from the beginning of their course. As numbers on the course grew, it became impossible to accommodate the whole student group at the same time. As a result, this part of the course moved to schools with their own swimming pools. At the same time, the use of more schools with students split into smaller groups led to the reintroduction of games teaching to this Autumn term experience.

At this stage in the development of the course, the typical programme for a PGCE student would have included one morning spent teaching swimming to pupils from two different classes followed by a seminar on theory and practice of swimming teaching. A second morning would be spent in a different school assisting with the teaching of either a gymnastics or a dance lesson and team teaching a games lesson.

The aims of this part of the course had also evolved over the years. Initially, with small numbers of students and fairly large groups of pupils, management issues had been stressed and students had been encouraged to look at basic strategies such as positioning for effective observation of the whole class, giving feedback to groups and to individuals in order to sustain motivation, organising groups, managing lesson transitions and so on. They had completed observation sheets on their peers which became the focus for post-lesson discussion. This was very much in the tradition of micro teaching adapted to our circumstances. At the time, considerable work on the observation and analysis of work in PE was being carried out especially in the USA (Siedentop 1983), but also in this country (Butterworth 1989). Latterly this had been rethought for two reasons. First, students seemed to receive plenty of help on class management from the departments with which they were placed later in the course. Second, we had begun to have doubts about the extent to which we were promoting the reflective practice which underpinned our course philosophy. Faced with students making judgements on their peers made in the light of their own, inevitably limited experience, it was tempting to impose our own judgements and standards on the group. We wondered whether we were actually encouraging or stifling reflection. On the other hand, if we withheld our judgements, were we compromising the development of competent practice? The focus thus shifted to pupil learning with a strong emphasis upon thinking about what pupils had learned rather than simply on what they had done during the lesson. This stress on a more considered reflection in relation to pupil learning enabled students to establish, early on in their course, the link between lesson planning and evaluation and pupil learning.

Responding to changing needs

The recent redesigning of the PGCE course was carried out by university staff and a group of teachers from partner schools. A number of these teachers had been involved in the school-based work carried out during the Autumn term and had viewed the experience in a very positive light from both student and pupil viewpoints. Because this part of the course was valued so highly, it was suggested and agreed that it be retained in the new structure. The proposed structure for the Autumn term appeared to provide a four week slot for the proposed work which meant that students would be able to teach a series of lessons. This would enable them to get to know the pupils and encourage them to provide progressive experiences. Questions then focused on the purposes of the school-based sessions and the activities to be taught.

It had already been agreed that the university should be responsible for introducing students to planning and evaluating lessons so the series of lessons to be taught during this four weeks became an obvious vehicle for work on planning and evaluation. Indeed, plans and evaluations for the four weeks became one of the students' assessed pieces of work for the term. In addition to this purpose, the school-based work was also seen as an ideal opportunity to reinforce, in a realistic setting, the practical workshops carried out at the university during the early stages of the course. Because students would be working with small groups of pupils there would also be the chance to concentrate on teaching and learning, as opposed to organisation and control.

With purposes identified, it was agreed that, given the activity areas currently within the National Curriculum at Key Stage 3 (games, gymnastics, dance, athletics, outdoor and adventurous activities and swimming if taught under one of the other headings), gymnastics, dance and water-based work should be given priority. The rationale for this was that dance provision in schools was very uneven, especially for boys, and that it was important that all students should have the opportunity to work with pupils who had the benefit of high quality teaching in this area. Similar reasons were advanced for the inclusion of gymnastics. Water-based activity was included because opportunities for teaching this are clearly facility-dependent and only a relatively small proportion of partner schools had swimming pools.

When putting this plan into action, students were taken to work in school in a group of sixteen. They worked with two parallel classes, so that there were eight students with each pupil group. Timetabling within the school enabled one group to be involved with a gymnastics lesson followed by dance and the other group to work with dance first and then gymnastics. For both gymnastics and dance lessons the 'usual' teacher remained with the class so that both tutor and teacher were able to observe the lesson and participate fully in the debrief which followed each week. For the first lesson either the teacher or the tutor led the activity to varying degrees to give the students an opportunity to observe the pupils they were about to teach and to get a feel for the work being carried out.

In one school, in gymnastics the tutor and teacher decided that the students would help pupils with sequence work, which would include lcarning of vaulting activities which could then be put into the sequence. Students worked in pairs with those less confident of their gymnastics knowledge paired with someone more confident. Each pair had a quarter of the working space and five or six pupils. The pupils were Year 8, mixed ability and mixed sex, but including a number of pupils who attended the local gymnastics club. In the second school students worked individually with a group of two or three Year 7 pupils, a mixed ability group of boys.

Dance lessons were carried out with classes similar to those for gymnastics, i.e. in one school, a Year 8 mixed sex, mixed ability group and in the second school a single sex (girls) mixed ability Year 7 group. In both cases students worked in pairs with groups of five or six pupils. A common theme of 'Conflict and Co-operation' ran through the dance work, although in one of the schools the students were working with pupils who were in the latter stages of an established unit of work whilst in the other school they were able to develop ideas from scratch. Parity of experience was not unduly hampered as the focus within both schools was centred on the expression of emotions related to the theme.

In swimming, the situation was rather different. The school involved had its own pool, which meant that it was possible for sixteen students to teach simultaneously. Some students had experience of teaching children to swim and had taken governing body qualifications in this activity prior to the start of the course. They were generally more confident in this activity than in the other two. For these lessons, the tutor worked with the students on the detailed planning of the content and led the debrief afterwards.

Reflections on the First Year

In addition to our own discussions about the successes of the work and about issues raised, we talked to the students and to the teachers involved about how they felt about the impact of this series of lessons on all involved.

Pupils

The opportunity to work in small groups and to receive individual attention benefited all pupils but was a particular bonus for some individuals and groups. For example one Year 7 boy was unable to perform any of the gymnastics skills which might be expected of a pupil of his age. He needed constant attention and help to improve his confidence and to encourage him to attempt very simple activities. A group which gained particular benefit was a small number of non-swimmers. The view of their class teacher was that they gained more than any other pupils as might be expected. Not only did the intensive teaching pay dividends because of the constant individual feedback and carefully targeted tasks, but, equally important, the pupils were not embarrassed because the numbers of 'teachers' meant that other members of the class were too busy to take any notice of them! Their teacher felt that this opportunity to learn without the self-consciousness which was often present during routine lessons was a major factor in the progress made.

In the dance context a number of children whose motivation was questioned were seen to thrive on the constant attention from 'their teacher'. It was also interesting to see that the pupils in the dance groups saw themselves as 'the group who had the students working with them' and continued to refer to this 'status' for some time after the lessons had finished. At the same time, the pupils gained in self-esteem and feelings of importance because they had been 'chosen' to work with the students. This was echoed, albeit in a slightly different way, in swimming where the pupils identified very much with 'their teacher' and appreciated the attention which they received. They were highly motivated to try to please the person whom they saw as 'theirs'. This sense of ownership seemed to be very important to them.

In several ways pupils had opportunities which they would probably not have had without the presence of the students. While the pupils would normally have been introduced to apparatus work involving flight within their gymnastics unit of work, opportunities to try the various vaulting possibilities were inevitably restricted. Able pupils who had the expertise and the confidence to perform without assistance were able to practise and refine their chosen activities, but many others simply did not have the opportunity to try. Through working with the students in this way, the pupils not only benefited from working in groups of three or four with their teacher, but their learning opportunities were extended because the teacher pupil ratio enabled all to attempt activities which were often restricted to the more able. With a supporter both to give confidence and to assist physically if needed and with apparatus at a height of the pupils' choosing most pupils were keen to attempt a variety of vaults.

In both gymnastics and dance the quality of the work produced improved because of the constant presence of a 'teacher' to give feedback, ask questions or encourage. Their class teacher also felt that at the same time as supporting pupil learning very effectively, the students' presence as 'outsiders' meant that pupils gained a feeling of 'performing' which was not generally present when they were working solely with one teacher. Pupil involvement in planning and evaluation was also enhanced by the constant presence of a 'teacher' to reinforce this aspect of the work and also to ensure that all members of pupil groups were involved.

For some pupils this was their first experience of being taught physical education at secondary school by someone of the opposite sex. They had the experience of working in a situation where role models for pupils of either sex were present. No pupils had previously been taught dance by male teachers therefore this four week series of lesson had the potential to challenge their assumptions about expertise in particular activities.

Teachers

All the teachers appreciated the opportunity presented by this series of lessons to stand back and observe the pupils to an extent that was not normally possible. One commented on the advantages of being able to watch and register the strengths and weaknesses of individual pupils without the usual pressures of having to react instantly or cope with organisational matters. Another felt that the chance to watch individual pupils' responses to different tasks in greater detail than usual was a bonus.

Debriefing sessions inevitably involved wide ranging discussion with the students. During the second and third weeks of the course, in addition to the work described here, students spent one day in the school where they were later to undertake a three week placement. Inevitably there were many questions about whether the work which they had just been involved with would be applicable in a different school, with different pupils or with different age groups. The teachers therefore were not only asked to articulate aspects of their own teaching in the context of their own school but would also be encouraged by the students to speculate about possible adaptations to other contexts. Students also often asked questions about which the teacher had simply not thought which encouraged the teacher to revisit aspects of his or her own experience which had been forgotten for some time.

One of the teachers involved felt that the presence of the students had encouraged her to think through the focus of each lesson with greater clarity and had also produced more of a focus on issues about teaching and learning, especially those related to differentiation and teaching styles. The process of thinking these through and discussing them with the students had also promoted similar thought about work undertaken with other classes. Another teacher thought that reflecting on the ideas and practices which the students were using and considering their application when working with larger groups was beneficial for her own practice as was the opportunity to see some new ideas being tried out.

Students

One of the difficulties faced by PGCE PE students is that, while they will have gained their degree as a result of their academic performance, they will be expected to teach an almost wholly practical programme in schools at Key Stages 3 and 4. Moreover the practical components of undergraduate courses are highly variable. Most will therefore need to improve their subject knowledge in at least some of the National Curriculum activity areas. This was particularly important in gymnastics, which for many was an area of relative weakness and where there are many safety issues. One was the need to learn to support pupils physically in activities where there was an element of risk. It was also important in the dance area, where physical danger was less likely but where pupil learning could be severely limited by the student's own lack of knowledge. One answer to this is clearly to undertake some intensive remedial work at the university and this is done. However, particularly in gymnastics, students are far from the ideal age to be learning basic skills which means that they find it extremely difficult to envisage the problems which a typical pupil might encounter. They find it equally difficult to imagine pupils finding skills easy when they themselves have struggled with them!

Related to gaps in students' subject knowledge is the need to give them confidence in their ability to help children to learn. This has been one of the major benefits of this work in the students' eyes. Many of them commented in their own assessment of the four weeks that they now felt that they had enough confidence in gymnastics and dance to be able to teach larger groups. We have noticed that, since giving all students the opportunity to teach dance in the Autumn term, an increasing number of male students now ask for further experience during their Spring term placement.

With both a teacher and a tutor present for much of the time, help is instantly available should a student need it. Because a large number of students and pupils were sharing the same space, the difficulties which can arise when a student is teaching alone and a teacher wants to intervene do not arise. As one of the students said, 'I think that what we do here... which is small group practice, there's a lovely introduction, it's safe, it's interesting, the kids are very well resourced in small groups like that – the schools love having us.'

For all students in their early teaching attempts, classroom management is understandably a major issue. For those in challenging schools it may well remain a top priority for much of a placement. The experience of working, in the first instance, with small groups, enables them to focus their attention on what the pupils are actually learning, indeed on whether they are learning anything or simply repeating activities with which they are already familiar.

For all students this experience provided early practice in lesson planning. During discussions on how the course should develop to meet the requirements of Circular 9/92, the teachers involved expressed the view that students should be taught to plan lessons before beginning any block placements and that the university should have this responsibility. The lessons taught gave a relevance to students' planning which would have been far more difficult to achieve if this activity had simply been introduced during a seminar. Because students were working with small groups, they were able to be ambitious in their aims. This meant that their practice included planning for more than just physical performance. Pupil involvement in planning and evaluating could be introduced at an early stage as could broader issues such as health or personal and social related development.

Evaluating one's own teaching is something which experienced teachers take for granted but which students find extremely difficult. During a placement in an ideal world students would have the opportunity to have their thinking guided or encouraged by a competent mentor, immediately after a lesson, on a regular basis. Sadly this is rarely possible. The opportunity to sit down with the teacher and other students straight after the lesson and to discuss what had gone well or less well which this series of lessons facilitates, gives students practical help with the skills of reflection from a very early stage in their course. The group debrief enabled thinking about the lesson to be shared, making its evaluation a much richer experience than is possible when one or two students talk with a teacher or tutor. The fact that their lesson plans and evaluations are a required piece of coursework meant that they all received both guidance and detailed feedback before being asked to plan and evaluate during block placements.

The shortage of time for university-based teaching during the PGCE has always led to high levels of motivation and a certain sense of urgency about all coursework. The immediacy of the work with pupils added a further dimension to this through the very clear focus given to the work undertaken at the university. The knowledge that one needs to acquire sufficient knowledge and understanding to plan and teach a lesson the following week is a very powerful motivator at the start of a course! Teaching small groups of pupils for a whole lesson is also demanding because activity time is maximised when organisational factors are removed. As one teacher commented, students have to be absolutely 'on the ball' when working intensively with small numbers. The opportunity to constantly refer to student experience with specific pupils during subsequent university-based work enhances the learning process powerfully.

As noted earlier, part of the rationale for the activity choices for this work was the need to ensure some comparability of experience for all students. For some students this would be their only experience of teaching swimming during the whole year. For several, mainly male students, there was no other opportunity to teach dance. The quality of the dance work with which students were involved gave them a valuable insight into appropriate expectations of Year 8 pupils. One student commented that dance in the school had a value within PE which was unlike any of the other schools she visited. She felt that the facilities available together with specialist dance teaching led to a very positive attitude towards it within the school. Comparability was not simply about the activities involved. Students all taught both male and female pupils and both mixed and single sex groups.

Many different teaching skills are introduced through this work. Students discover that pupils often do exactly what they say (even when this is not what they meant) and exactly as they are shown, which means that important lessons are learned about the use of appropriate language and clear demonstrations. They also begin to learn about establishing effective relationships with pupils including the need to maintain a certain distance and to behave as a professional rather than as a student. However, in relation to the 'student status' often perceived as a drawback when working in school, it was interesting to note the positive response engendered among the pupils. They were proud of the fact that they had students working with them and, as a result, conferred high status on the student group. For the students who later returned to that school for two block placements, being described as a student carried none of the negative connotations which applied in some other schools. Without the pressures of managing large groups they are able to gain an early awareness of individual differences not only in ability but also in response to particular tasks or learning approaches. At the same time, the presence of up to eight students, each teaching two or three pupils meant that through watching other groups performing, insight was gained into the learning of the whole class as well as the student's own pupil group.

Conclusions

We have found that the work in the Autumn term provides a safe, supported introduction to teaching for all students. It gives all experience of several different activity areas in a number of different schools. It promotes a focus upon teaching and learning at a very early stage in the course by removing the necessity to organise large groups. While challenging student thinking at every stage, it also develops both competence and, equally important at this stage, confidence which gives a good foundation upon which subsequent work can build. In ensuring that all students receive a basic common experience this part of the course also capitalises upon the economies of scale which operate through enabling students to learn about selected aspects of teaching in large groups rather than in individual schools singly or in pairs. Our students have been very conscious of the time constraints upon teachers even with some money going into schools to support work with students. 'There is no way that she's got time to try to prepare you to teach, she can't give you practices in everything you're likely to come across, but the university does.' This comment by one of the students sums up the view of many and also of many of the mentors.

This work can also be an effective form of professional development for the mentors involved. The opportunity to discuss professional matters, even for a limited time, with what one teacher described as a 'neutral' professional colleague was valued. Development of mentoring skills is also possible in that the teachers involved are engaged in some of the activities which McIntyre and Hagger describe as 'developed mentoring'. (McIntyre and Hagger 1993). These include collaborative teaching, in this case involving students, teachers and tutors; giving students access to the craft knowledge of experienced teachers; discussing learner-teachers' ideas; and managing beginning teachers' learning opportunities.

Collaborative teaching was a feature of the dance and gymnastics work in the early stages when teacher and tutor would lead a part of the lesson, agreed in advance with the students who would then teach other agreed sections. Burn (in Wilkin 1992) suggests that while collaborative teaching is one element within a teacher training programme, it does have an extremely useful role to play especially early on in the course when it can enable students to come to terms with 'real teaching' while remaining in a protected environment.

The teachers were frequently challenged, as were the tutors, by student questions which related not only to the lesson which they had just taught but ranged over many wider issues. This demanded both an articulation of the teacher's own knowledge and also encouraging discussion of the students' own ideas.

The discussions which took place between tutors and teachers in the process of setting up this work and agreeing its precise focus involved all the teachers in the management of student learning opportunities, albeit on a small scale. During the course of the four weeks the teachers became involved with larger groups of students than they would normally meet during the course of a block placement which enabled them to extend their experience of students and to appreciate the range of expertise, confidence and competence with which students begin their PGCE year.

Review of this year's experience reinforces our view that this work remains worthwhile. In the context of partnership it is cost effective – an important consideration when resources are scarce – and, far more important, produces identifiable benefits to all involved. We hope that the greater contact between higher education tutors and teachers (albeit only a proportion of our mentors) has opened up possibilities for dialogue and for a greater consistency of approach to work with students. We will be following this up as the work continues to develop.

CHAPTER 9

Partnership in Religious Education: school-based method work

In this chapter the experience of partnership in Religious Education between the School of Education and five Birmingham schools is described and evaluated. The account focuses on school-based method work taking place on six half days in the Autumn term and four half days and one full day in the Summer term. The PGCE RE course at the University of Birmingham has had a school-based element (called the Team-Teaching Exercise) in its method work during the Autumn term for over twenty years so the Circular 9/92 requirement did not require too radical a change in its mode of operation. What it did require was an extension of this practice to the equivalent of six whole days. However, although the five schools selected for this purpose had been similarly involved for many years previously, it was important that the opportunity should be taken for a critical review of past practice and a careful consideration of how to relate work done in schools to the acquisition of those competences identified in Circular 9/92. Consequently a teachers' working group, made up of the Heads of RE from each of the five schools and the university tutor, was set up and a programme of meetings arranged during the 1992–93 academic year in readiness for the implementation of a new course in September 1993.

Tutor and mentors planning the Team-Teaching experience

In previous years the Team-Teaching Exercise had been seen as a way of giving students a gentle introduction to teaching at the beginning of the Autumn term prior to their three week School Placement which occurred, usually, immediately after half term. Allowing for a week's induction at the beginning of the course this meant that teams of four students would be in schools for half a day each week for four weeks. After their three week School Placement they would return to their 'Team Teaching School' for half a day for two further weeks, ending the experience just prior to the end of the Autumn term. In the event, this same pattern was adopted for the 1993–94 course.[1]

In the past, the emphasis of the Team-Teaching Exercise had been placed on the acquisition of 'initial teaching skills', the assumption being that student teachers of RE must acquire proficiency in skills common to the act of teaching itself before acquiring skills which might be said to be peculiar to teaching RE. Both types of skill were believed to be best acquired through analysing practice rather than expecting students to translate theory into practice. It was felt by the teachers' working group that this assumption was sound and that the checklist for the evaluation of initial teaching skills remained a valuable tool for this purpose (see Appendix).

The group felt, however, that on the occasion of their first half day, teams should make use of a simplified schedule which would provide guided observation of the teacher teaching the classes that they would subsequently be teaching. Consequently the group produced a document entitled 'Watching the teacher', requiring written comments to be made against the following headings: reception/registration; use of voice; instructions; use of board/OHP; layout of classroom; teaching materials; atmosphere; comfort; control techniques; dismissal of pupils; interaction (Figure 9.1). A second observation schedule, for use on the second half day, was produced entitled 'Spot the Structure'. (Figure 9.2) This emphasised the importance of the link between change of activity and change of pace and required students to note the time of changes made and how the lesson developed. Teachers ensured that the lessons observed did not all conform to a similar pattern, so, for example, they comprised a mixture of formal, class lessons and lessons using groups and active learning strategies.

Two further schedules were produced: a Lesson Structure Plan and a Lesson Delivery Plan, the latter introducing the concept of evaluation of teaching (Figures 9.3 and 9.4). The five teachers involved in the scheme – technically 'mentors' – were encouraged to use the plans for preparing those lessons that the students would observe. Afterwards the plans were used by the teams in the preparation of their own lessons, and some students continued to use the same plans for their teaching practice later in the year. There was no agreed subject content for the lessons, each school being free to continue with whatever came next in the RE syllabus.

---

[1] In consultation with students, the teachers' working group has now changed this pattern to two half days and two full days, all before the three week School Placement in the Autumn term.

Figure 9.1

WATCHING...the teacher!   PGCE – RE

What?	Comments
Reception/ Registration	
Use of voice	
Instructions	
Use of board/OHP	
Layout of classroom	
Teaching materials	
Atmosphere	
Comfort	
Control techniques	
Dismissal of pupils	
Interaction	

Your name.. Date...........................

Figure 9.2

SPOT...the structure! **PGCE – RE**

Timing	Lesson development
—	
—	
—	
—	
—	
—	
—	
—	
—	
—	
—	
—	
—	
—	
—	
—	
—	
—	
—	

Your name.. Date...........................

There was agreement, however, that in the Autumn term the focus of the work with students would be on guided observation (sometimes of each other, using the initial teaching skills checklist), recognition of strategies of class control, identifying lesson structures/teaching strategies appropriate to teaching the whole class, groups, pairs and individuals, and the selection and use of resources. Mentors would be present for the lessons, but would not necessarily teach, and would provide a debrief afterwards, preferably written. The university tutor would visit two teams per week and would also provide a debrief. Additionally, video recording of the teams teaching would be made and these would be used in university sessions as a basis for discussion and comment on skill development.

Students preparing to teach in schools

Although guidance on lesson construction, including aim, objectives, learning activities and forms of assessment of learning was given by both mentors and the university tutor, each team of students had the responsibility of meeting in their own time to plan their lessons. This encouraged closer working relationships to develop among team members than would normally occur in a group of twenty students. Each member of each team was expected to play some part in each lesson, so careful attention had to be paid to the 'choreography' of team teaching. The effect of four students thinking co-operatively about how they were to teach a given area of content (which may or may not have been familiar to all or some of them) was to promote considerably more reflection on what they were trying to achieve and how to do so than is normally the case when a student prepares a lesson on his or her own. Additionally, the learning situations that were devised by this process generally displayed a greater degree of imagination, were more appropriately structured (sometimes just because they wanted to ensure that all four had their own distinctive contribution!), were more accurate in their treatment of content and had a greater interest value to the pupils. The fact that lessons were also being videoed with the possibility of playback to the whole group also increased motivation for conscientious application at the planning stage.

Subject content covered during six half day team teaching experiences in the five schools included: Year 7 – Early Religion (Stone Age burial; Stonehenge; Animism; Aboriginal beliefs about the Dreamtime); Moses; The Exodus; The Ten Plagues; Year 8 – Diwali; Christmas decorations in a Church; Christian Symbols; Sabbath in the Synagogue and Home; Year 9 – Rites of Passage (Infant Ceremonies; Coming of Age Ceremonies;

Figure 9.3

LESSON STRUCTURE PLAN   PGCE – RE

Title:		Date	Form/class	No.of pupils	Ability	Period(s)	Length

Aim/Overview

Objectives

to know about

to understand

to think about/reflect upon

Sequence of activities

Assessment of learning

Classroom organisation

Resources

Figure 9.4

LESSON DELIVERY PLAN PGCE – RE

Sequence of activities	Proposed timing

Evaluation of teaching

Page...............of...............

Marriage Ceremonies); Year 10 – GCSE Sikhism (The Guru Granth Sahib, Worship, Amrit); Year 11 – PSE (Careers); Upper Sixth: A Level GCE Religious Studies – Ethical Issues (Christian and Muslim perspectives on The Sanctity of Life, Suicide, Euthanasia). This is fairly typical content that is found in most contemporary RE syllabuses, but it would be unusual to find any one student whose initial degree course in Theology or Religious Studies had equipped them to feel confident that they could teach all of it. The pooling of knowledge facilitated by working in teams thus enabled students to extend their knowledge base quite rapidly and to do so within the context of thinking about its educational worth and application. This was an important learning experience, therefore, which had direct relevance to their professional development.

Students acquiring initial teaching skills in schools

An essential part of the experience was for each student to write a reflective evaluation of each lesson in which they participated, using the checklist of initial teaching skills. What follows are extracts from one student's evaluation of her own contribution to two lessons on 'Marriage' that a team taught to a Year 9 class, early in the Autumn term.

> I thought the lessons went well on the whole, with the second lesson an improvement on the first. I was pleased with my teaching, although there were one or two points I will need to improve on: 'presence' – I will try to come forward more often. I think the children enjoyed the lesson as when the bell went they didn't start packing away. This was, I presume, because of their interest in the lesson. They were very eager to participate both in the lesson and in the group discussions. They learnt about the solemnity of marriage vows and responsibility involved in marriage. Their understanding was borne out by their responses to the 'marriage problems' activities which we had devised. Today's lessons were more enjoyable for myself because I relaxed more and was able to use humour. Points for improvement are:
>
> Use of chalkboard: I should write the homework on the board.
>
> Voice: I did use my voice for dramatic effect in the roleplay but my instructions need to be clearer and repeated.
>
> Exposition of content: I was enthusiastic and interesting; I checked their understanding frequently; I used praise; I included at least five

examples to illustrate issues; I made use of drawings, worksheets, pictures, cards and acting.

Questioning: I used questions with difficult pupils as a method of class control; I repeated a pupil's answer when it was very good; I thought up some questions 'on the spot' but most were prepared.

Teaching aids: I used cards with typed writing, bold and neat.

Organisation: We divided them into groups ourselves; some had to be cajoled; I scanned the classroom frequently and gave individuals attention when they needed it.

Class Control: We were present before the pupils arrived and I stood by the door; we established quiet before beginning; the lesson started with pupils being asked to write down their own ideas; we used praise and avoided confrontations; we had a procedure for dismissing the class.

What I learned:

Don't use green OHP pens!
Focused questions are better than general ones.
Bring in personal experience and class experience.
Use books and tapes but keep them short and get a lot of feedback from the class.
Have the class involved in an activity early on.
Be humorous, lively and interesting.
Use less materials and draw more out of the children. *(Amanda)*

These comments[2] bear out that, initially, students recognise the need to acquire teaching skills which have general applicability and are not subject-specific. In her evaluation the student makes no direct references to the difficulties presented by the topic – Marriage. The subject-specific concerns, including bringing these within a framework of the broad, educational concerns of RE, may need, therefore, to be introduced as part of the discussion of the lesson with mentor or university tutor. Indeed, the value of having a videoed record of the lesson is to help students who have participated in it to stand back from the experience and to view it more objectively, including their treatment of subject content. Such video recorded evidence also enables all students in the whole RE group to benefit from the discussion.

---

[2] I am grateful to the PGCE RE students of the 1993/1994 academic year for their permission to quote extracts from their files recording the team-teaching experience.

Building on the Team-Teaching experience in the University

A group of Religious Studies graduates discussing RE in a university seminar room can easily slip into an unrealistic and over-idealistic view of their subject. But when discussion arises from direct confrontation with the realities of classroom life there vividly before them on the TV screen – mixed ability, multi-faith classes; pupils with no direct links with institutional religion; some pupils alienated from both school and religion, etc – students cannot avoid grappling with the key issues that face each and every one of them. These appraisal sessions with the university tutor, therefore, do not consist of passive observation of lessons; key moments in the lesson are identified, short teaching sequences are re-run, alternative responses to those given at the time to pupils' questions or comments are formulated, new objectives, activities and emphases are suggested, and alternative control techniques considered. In short, the video provides the stimulus for students to 're-process' the lesson they have taught and in so doing to recognise that successful RE teaching depends on the teacher's ability to design learning experiences which are best able to promote interaction between pupils and what they are learning about. For example, learning situations which encourage pupils to ask questions about the content they are studying rather than answer questions on the content; learning situations which require pupils to apply their knowledge of the beliefs and values of different religions to an understanding of themselves; learning situations which prompt pupils to appraise their own beliefs and values, not merely learn about those of others. In helping students to recognise such concerns as these as fundamental to the religious education of pupils, the video also provides the stimulus for the students themselves to re-appraise and re-evaluate their own beliefs and values and so further their own religious education.

A partnership in promoting competences

With regard to the development of competences identified in Circular 9/92, the team teaching arrangement in the Autumn term was designed to concentrate on approximately twelve of these. *Subject Knowledge*: although there was an obvious contribution to this from work with mentors, an understanding of the knowledge, concepts and skills of RE, as indicated above, and knowledge of the application of the National Curriculum formula to RE, as evident in new Agreed Syllabuses, came from evaluative sessions in the university. Such understanding was substantially developed by teaching practice during the Spring term and by a written assignment in the Summer term. *Subject Application*: the existence of a true partnership between mentors and the university tutor was particularly evident with regard to producing coherent lesson plans, employing a range of teaching strategies appropriate to the age, ability and attainment level of pupils, presenting subject content in clear language and in a stimulating manner and demonstrating the ability to select and use appropriate resources, including information technology.

Mentors, on the other hand, took the main responsibility for Class Management, ensuring that students were helped to decide when teaching the whole class, groups, pairs or individuals was appropriate, how to create and maintain a purposeful and orderly environment, how to devise and use appropriate rewards and sanctions to maintain an effective learning environment, and how to maintain pupils' interest and motivation.

Under the heading of Further Professional Development, mentors and the university tutor shared the responsibility for establishing an awareness of individual differences, including social, psychological, developmental and cultural dimensions and promoting a self-critical approach to diagnosing and evaluating pupils' learning. The latter was substantially extended through work undertaken in the Summer term.

Students' end of the Autumn term evaluations of their experience

Students were encouraged to evaluate the Autumn term team teaching experience after their sixth half day, and they all wrote extensively, and in the main, enthusiastically about it. Three examples are:

I think working as a team can be very productive and helpful both for the pupils and ourselves. *(Justine)*

I have enjoyed working in my team teaching group and feel I have got on well with all the members of the group....The mentor was very helpful and supportive in everything we did. She was willing to talk to us and go over what we did, saying what was positive and giving us ways in which we could improve some of the things we did....I think it has been a positive experience and have found that I have learnt a lot from it. *(Angela)*

I began the exercise of 'team teaching' with a certain amount of apprehension but it turned out to be a thoroughly enjoyable and very useful exercise in many ways. Firstly, I have enjoyed the challenge of teaching in a team; secondly, I have enjoyed watching colleagues work, seeing occasional mistakes and gaining insights through them into teaching; thirdly, the school, with its pupils from many different ethnic and religious backgrounds, has provided a wonderful contrast to the school where I undertook my three week placement; fourthly, I have been intellectually challenged by the plethora of subjects I have had to teach, and also challenged to discover and develop a variety of classroom control techniques. I have also been supported and encouraged by my 'team' colleagues as well as by mentors and tutors. The net result of all this is a feeling that I can become a teacher, cope with the subjects that will need to be taught, control a class and, most importantly, enjoy it all! *(Neil)*

Team teaching in the Summer term

The team teaching arrangement for the Summer term had a different focus. Teams returned to their team teaching schools for half a day a week for four weeks then, in the week following half term, some of the pupils from each school, the students and their mentors came to the university for a whole day to present and display the work they had undertaken together. As before, there was no common subject content, each school proceeded with its normal curriculum. The teachers' working group had agreed, however, that the focus of the time in school would be on methods of teaching RE, and had suggested: exploring religious buildings; using story, drama, roleplay and dance; making a video, or games and simulations; and preparing an act of collective worship. In terms of the Circular 9/92 competences the focus permitted a further contribution from mentors to Subject Application and Class Management but with an additional contribution, under Further Professional Development, to the ability to recognise diversity of talent and the ability to identify special educational needs or learning difficulties. In the event, especially as a consequence of the final day of presentation and display, the experience did enhance competences under Assessment, Recording and Reporting of pupils' progress, namely to judge how well each pupil performs against the standard expected of a pupil of that age.

Again, the variety of subject content covered by the teams was considerable. It included: Year 7 – The Ten Plagues and the themes from Exodus; the trial and crucifixion of Jesus; the miracles and parables of Jesus; Year 8 – making a stained glass window; a religious buildings 'monopoly' game; Islamic calligraphy, pictures and stories of Hindu deities, places of pilgrimage, religious dress in Buddhism, Christianity and Islam; Year 10 – GSCE Religious Studies coursework – making a video of the life and work of three local churches; compiling wordprocessed illustrated booklets on aspects of worship. One Year 8 group also prepared an act of collective worship.

A day in the university with pupils, students and mentors

In the Summer term the students found themselves working mainly with small groups of pupils alongside their mentors. Some of them found this style of working an anticlimax after their Spring term teaching practice:

> I did not find team teaching as valuable as I did in the Autumn term. After a term on teaching practice developing personal teaching styles, it is difficult to adapt back to the team teaching situation... Angela, Karen and I flitted between groups and I personally felt more like a teaching assistant than an actual teacher! *(Justine)*

Despite this, the amount and quality of work that came out of the four half days was impressive. Even more gratifying, the presentation day in the university confounded the scepticism that had begun to emerge and proved to be a very successful occasion.

> I was very impressed by the work done by the other schools and also the behaviour and courage of the pupils, some of whom were only in Year 7. *(Kirsty)*

> We displayed all their work on the boards. We were very pleased with the standard of work they had produced. They spoke very well. They had really risen to the occasion. *(Angela)*

> Our three spokespersons were exceptional; they were articulate, interesting and explained very well what we had been doing with them in the last four lessons. They had obviously understood the concepts and it was clear that we had met the objectives we had addressed in the way they answered the questions. *(Caroline)*

> I was pleasantly surprised to discover how well the university day went and was very pleased with how well the pupils from 7L presented their project. This day was extremely valuable. *(Richard)*

> In discussion, all pupils showed that they had a good grasp of the issues that they were addressing and I feel that this project has been a positive experience for them. *(Jason)*

> The three girls were a credit to their school as well as to us. As we interviewed the pupils we tried to draw the responses from them rather

than leap in with an elaboration of the answer after their initial response. I was delighted with the level of understanding that all three pupils showed. *(Stephen)*

The benefits of the partnership to pupils and students

It is significant that the Headteacher of one of the participating schools in the school-based work asked, after the completion of the course, how the pupils in his school had gained from the school's involvement in the partnership. His Head of Department was of the view that the RE Department – one of the best in the region – valued its links with the university for a number of reasons. Although in his case, where there was more than one specialist in the Department, re-appraisal of the curriculum and teaching strategies was an ongoing activity, it was beneficial to him and his staff to be involved very directly with teacher training because of the added impetus that this gave to critical self-assessment. For example, the task of inducting students into skills often led to reflection on their own practices and an awareness of areas in which improvements could be made. He felt that the quality of teaching and learning was enhanced by the presence of students in the classroom working with the teacher, not merely because of the additional attention that individual pupils could receive, but because of the desire to ensure that the students witnessed the best of good practice and did so within an atmosphere of professional commitment and enthusiasm for the subject. Involvement, however, did represent a considerable commitment of time and effort, often outside normal teaching times. It is interesting to note that in this school, where a group of Year 10 GCSE pupils made three separate videos of the life and work of three local churches, both pupils and students gave freely of time after school and at weekends to complete this work. Without the involvement of students it is unlikely that such an ambitious, but educationally desirable project could have been attempted, with such excellent results.

One of the other schools involved has a large number of pupils with special educational needs, many of them with a language other than English as their mother tongue. Additionally, some of the pupils have emotional and behavioural problems. In this school, the presence of a team of students enabled learning support to be given on an unprecedented scale. Indeed, the project undertaken in the Summer term was only brought to its very successful outcome as a result of the mentor, students and pupils being prepared to work during some lunchtimes and after school. In contrast to fears expressed by some critics that the presence of students in schools means that pupils will be less well taught,

108

this experience suggests that the opposite is the case.

The value of any partnership consists of the different but complementary contributions that each of the partners can offer. From this description it should be apparent that what the schools offered was an initiation into good practice, particularly in terms of promoting those competences included under the heading of Classroom Management, and generally in terms of Subject Application. If there was a common weakness in the five schools it lay in the area of assessment – both of the quality of pupils' learning and in the assessment of student performance.

RE has been slow nationally to put in place an effective system of statements of attainment and end of key stage statements; this, of course, reflects the fact that it is not a National Curriculum subject and is locally determined through LEA Agreed Syllabuses. In Birmingham the 1975 Agreed Syllabus is still to be revised and schools have not had the benefit of a document based on the more recent National Curriculum pattern. It is not surprising, therefore, that schools in the partnership could only make a limited contribution to teaching students how to judge how well each pupil performs against the standard expected of a pupil that age. One of the advantages of having the presentation day was the discussion about standards that it provoked afterwards!

Equally, mentors in schools have limited experience of what standards of performance might reasonably be expected of a PGCE RE student both before, during and after teaching practice. Experience of students in their own school, even when spread over several years, cannot be expected to yield the same understanding that a university tutor has as a result of observing and working with many different students in many different schools. This moderating role of the university tutor remains crucial to ensure quality of teacher training. Additionally, students reported that, despite the excellence of the support they received from their mentors, including those in the teaching practice schools, not all were able to write a constructively critical critique of their lessons. It is easy for mentors to underestimate the importance of the written critique as a teaching strategy in the training of teachers. Critiques provided by some mentors were far too general – either negatively or positively. The careful analysis of performance is not something that can be done without training and experience and it lies at the heart of the distinctive contribution that the university tutor makes to the partnership.

Conclusion

There has been a significant shift in the understanding of partnership as a consequence of recent legislative changes in teacher training. As indicated at the beginning of this chapter, there is a long history of PGCE RE students working in schools as a part of their method course. However, the basis of that earlier arrangement was much more about the university 'borrowing' classes of pupils for half a day a week for students to practise on, with most of the direction and supervision of the experience falling to the university tutor. The present partnership is almost the reverse. It is no longer the pupils that are 'borrowed' but the students! Teachers as mentors now have an opportunity, and a responsibility, to balance the needs of pupils with those of the students and to create a meaningful learning experience for both, with the emphasis on good practice which ensures quality of learning and optimum levels of achievement. The university shares in this experience but no longer directs it. A professional partnership is evolving to the benefit of all.

CHAPTER 10

Partnership in Science: the early days in schools

Introduction

Partnerships between schools and HEIs have been developing since the 1980s (DES/HMI 1991) and have been given a further impetus by Circular 9/92 (DfE 1992). In all the various models of partnership there seems to be an underlying uneasiness with the theory–practice divide. Time spent in HEIs is often seen by students and teachers as 'theory laden' (Dunne, Lock and Soares, forthcoming) while the time spent in schools, providing the much needed practice to develop competences, does not always allow time to step back and reflect on the plethora of experiences students encounter.

During the block practices in schools and during the university-based work one or other of the partners plays the leading role and it is mainly during the serial practice that a more equal partnership is likely. The part of the serial practice addressed here involved two groups of science students spending three days in a school, in the first term of their training, following a programme planned and organised by a science mentor and a university tutor, and delivered jointly with contributions from other teachers in the school. It is approaches such as this that are said to be of benefit to all parties concerned in the partnership.

> When teachers plan students' programmes with tutors and join in when the students' lessons are reviewed and when ideas and resources are shared, all the participants benefit. (DES/HMI 1991, p.23)

The advantages of serial practice as described in the preceding paragraph are usually obvious but it is often assumed that 'having students' is only of direct benefit to teachers once they have gained sufficient competence in teaching and can be left to 'get on with it', thus relieving teachers of the classes they would be teaching, and providing valuable 'space' for teachers. This part of the chapter describes how the early part of the serial practice was planned and organised, and hopes to provide evidence, that an involvement with student teachers even at an early stage of their training, in the first six weeks, can be of benefit to pupils and teachers as well as enhance the quality of training students.

The choice of school for this phase was determined by several factors:
- a science teacher who was familiar with the overall structure of the course;
- a science teacher who was prepared to work with the university tutor in planning and delivering the programme in this phase, the teacher-tutor;
- a department where several staff would be willing to work with students in their classes at this early stage of their training;
- a department where several classes would be available at times that did not clash with the students' other timetable commitments;
- a school that could accommodate sixteen students and their tutor;
- a school that was within a reasonable distance from the university.

If someone were to suggest to you that sixteen students who were all training to be science teachers would be coming to work with your department all at the same time, how would you respond? We suspect that many initial reactions would be slightly incredulous, but this is what has been planned and implemented in two Birmingham schools.

The main aim of the serial practice in the initial stages of the course, determined by a group of science mentors and tutors, was to provide student teachers with a gradual immersion into classroom practice with the following objectives in mind:
- to complement the issues addressed on the university-based part of the course;
- to feed into the university-based parts of the course;
- to provide experience of working with small groups of pupils in science;
- to plan, teach and evaluate parts of lessons identified by the teachers;
- to provide opportunities to develop observation and evaluation skills;
- to help to identify students' particular strengths and needs;
- to reflect on what it means to be a science teacher;
- to enjoy the experience.

The following sections of this chapter describe and evaluate how the different experiences of two groups of science students in two partnership schools (School A and School B) worked to the benefit of students and teachers.

School A

The serial practice in School A was carried out in October/November 1993. School A is a maintained, coeducational, 11–18, comprehensive school located in inner city Birmingham. With a roll of 1,300 pupils, this multicultural school has had strong links with the university over a number of years leading on from a large commitment to taking students on teaching practice, through helping to develop the partnership scheme and implementing it in its first year. Eleven members of a seventy-two strong staff teach in the science department and it was with these colleagues that sixteen science student teachers, two students to each of eight teachers, were located for part of three days of serial practice discussed in this section.

The mentor located in the science department had been heavily involved in developing the content, structure and methods to be used in the serial practice. This led to a 'typical' day of serial practice having the following components:

9.00-10.15 Tutor-led session on questioning techniques

10.15-10.45 Preparation for observing teaching (questioning skills)

11.00-11.45 Observing teachers (lesson 3)

11.45-12.30 Preparation by students for tutorial

12.30- 1.30 Lunch break

1.30- 2.15 Teaching with teachers (lesson 5)

2.15- 3.30 Student-led tutorial based on investigations carried out in lesson observation (mentor/tutor present)

3.30- 4.30 Mentor/tutor-led session on related topic (small group discussion)

With a structure such as this there was a clear theme to the day (questioning skills) and direct involvement in two lessons, two mentor/tutor-led sessions and two student-controlled activities. Such an arrangement provided for a busy but varied day.

For the activity to be successful at least eight teachers in the department had to be prepared to have a pair of students in two of their lessons on the same day of three consecutive weeks. Also the lessons had to be such that they would fit into the pattern of the day; lesson 3 and lesson 5. In general lesson 3 was designated as the lesson in which students would carry out observations of the teachers at work while in lesson 5 they would help with the teaching in an increasingly involved manner; *Week A* – working with individuals, *Week B* – small group work, *Week C* – teaching the whole class.

Money for teacher release time was not used to buy out from classroom time as this was seen as disruptive. Instead, each of the eight teachers involved gave time at morning break and in the lunch hour to briefing students about lessons they were about to observe, help with or teach. In addition, one or two teachers were involved with the sessions after the end of the school day.

If the project was to be successful, it was important that school staff were in full support of the project. Consequently, part of an INSET morning in September was given over to a briefing by the university tutor of the science department on the purpose of this activity. A significant element of this work was discussing the nature of the observation activities that it was proposed students would use in the teachers' lessons. As a consequence of this discussion, some proposed observation activities were modified; no proposed activity was rejected outright.

This was an important step in the exercise. Teachers were fully aware of what was proposed and why students were being asked to observe in such a structured manner. They were assured that in the student-led tutorial work based on the observations, anonymity was guaranteed. As a result of the activity ten staff agreed to be involved.

Classes from a range of years (7 to 12) were used and lesson content included biology, physics, chemistry and earth science. The teaching of whole classes in the third week meant that all students in the group got their first 'solo' experience as a pair on the same day. This was an event which, thanks to the expertise and support of normal class teachers, proved a positive and encouraging encounter for all students, teachers and pupils.

At the end of the third week of the exercise, the staff and students were separately asked to complete parallel questionnaires that explored their attitudes to the exercise and the advantages and disadvantages of being observed/observing and teaching/helping with teaching and learning activities during the lessons involved. Responses to questionnaires were later discussed in a departmental meeting (teachers) and at a debrief session at the university (students).

The questionnaire asked whether the students/teachers had enjoyed this activity or not and followed this up with questions which asked them to write down any advantages and disadvantages to observing. All teachers and students said they enjoyed this exercise and then qualified this by commenting on particularly successful elements and raising aspects that could be improved if the exercise was to be repeated in the following year. Among the advantages mentioned by teachers were that it was good preparation for appraisal and OFSTED. Three said it made them think more about their lessons and plan them more thoroughly while others were keen to make a 'good impression'. Two teachers were not keen on being observed but felt that if it helped students then it was acceptable. Students were discreet with their observations and any teachers who asked were shown the data that had been collected.

Students welcomed the experience of working with and observing different teachers as well as enjoying the 'real lessons'. Two found observation activities boring after a while, '...especially with good teachers' – the observation activity was possibly not sufficiently demanding.

Although all teachers and students responded by saying they had enjoyed this activity, there were both positive and negative points raised. Teachers felt it was helpful to pupils to have more help and attention. They also mentioned the advantages of new faces and new ideas. One teacher, however, found that it was disruptive with extra persons in the lab. Several teachers suggested that if the activity was repeated it would be better to build in more time to the programme where they could help students to plan lessons. These comments were made even though they would require the teachers to give up time in breaks, at lunchtime or after school.

Students thought it was good for putting ideas into practice, gave them a feel of what was involved and boosted their confidence. There was no consensus on whether there should be more such activity or whether it should have come earlier in the course than week 5. Students also wanted more time for liaison with teachers, and they found the written feedback on the lesson they had taught very helpful, constructive and supportive.

Six teachers said they would be pleased to repeat the exercise in 1994; one was uncertain, one did not respond. The same six teachers agreed that six consecutive weeks of such practice would be acceptable, i.e. extending the exercise to twice its current length. Students, in contrast, thought three weeks was about right. They found the days very intensive and tiring. More time was needed by some students for preparing to present and discuss data from observation lessons.

The technicians found it hard work in the week when students were responsible for teaching the whole class. The idea here was that students would take over and teach the lesson that the normal class teacher would have delivered. In practice, some students were less economic with equipment and resources than experienced teachers would have been, not an uncommon phenomenon when students are new to planning lessons. This experience led to the comments reported earlier, that teachers would welcome more time in which to help students plan lessons where more thorough discussion of, particularly equipment lists, would help ease the technicians' workload. However, the technicians found the new ideas and good quality, wordprocessed worksheets produced by students a valued addition to school resources.

There were unforeseen benefits that came from the work too. The teacher responsible for special needs heard of the observation work that students were doing and came to investigate. She had ended up using her own versions of some of these activities to help raise her colleagues' awareness of the implications for teaching pupils with special needs in their classes.

School B

The activities for the three days in school were planned and organised by the teacher-tutor and university tutor in order to meet the objectives of the serial practice described earlier. Students would spend some time in groups of four working with a particular class and teacher, as helpers and observers initially and extending to planning for and taking charge of a small activity. Some time would also be spent as a whole group of students, with the teacher-tutor and university tutor, addressing various 'theoretical' aspects of practical issues such as classroom management and discipline, safety and risk assessment, marking and assessment. It was decided, rightly or wrongly, that three whole days, after an initial settling in period for the students when some form of group identity developed, would benefit them; one double lesson would be spent in lessons with the rest of the day addressing other issues, including preparation and debriefing. The availability of supply cover for the teacher-tutor's timetable for the rest of the day was also an important factor as was the demand likely to be placed on technicians in the department.

The thought of five adults in a classroom gave rise to some anxiety in one teacher at first:

I wondered about having so many adults in the room and the possibility that delivering the content in this way would cause confusion. (Teacher A – 4 years teaching experience)

but was, on the whole, received positively,

I immediately thought of investigations. Practical work that I would normally shy away from became a possibility with difficult groups. (Teacher B, Head of Science).

It was important that the other teachers involved were prepared to enter into this arrangement, negotiated by the teacher-tutor and university tutor. The input required from the other contributing teachers included providing a lesson plan with certain 'signposts' for students to observe specifically, identifying activities that the groups of students take responsibility for delivering, and evaluating critical incidents at the end of the lesson also needed to be appreciated. As it was the first time that the teachers were involved in such an activity it was imperative to assure them that observations and evaluations were to be approached in the context of 'joint enquiries' leading to genuine discussion rather than being seen to be judgemental. The persuasive skill of the teacher-tutor needs to be mentioned here!

It was important that the serial practice was arranged with minimal disruption of staff and pupils, and to this end the serial practice had to fit in with the normal work of a particular class and teacher. The discontinuity and the lack of opportunity to build relationships with pupils and their teachers were unavoidable disadvantages of this approach but it was felt that these were outweighed by the advantages to students, working with small groups of pupils and having time to jointly prepare the trial activities.

What follows is a sample of the types of activities that students were involved in and the comments made by the teachers, when interviewed, on the benefits to pupils, themselves and the department.

The particular activities that each group of students undertook varied and depended on the class and topic being covered at the time of the visits; illustrative class practicals, investigations, and activities using IT were among those that featured during the three days. The advantages for the students included the opportunities to prepare collaboratively with the teacher and the university tutor, and then to teach small groups of pupils without the distractions that arise with whole class management issues, particularly at this stage.

It was a nice soft start to planning lessons, activities and practicals ... and with a difficult group this was made more manageable. It gave us (students) the opportunity to work as a group. (Student)

The collaborative approach, small group size and the available help of the teacher and tutor, encouraged students to take 'risks' and look for alternative ways in which to approach the objectives set by the teacher for the particular activity. Two examples will be used to illustrate this. In the first, the group of students was asked to give instructions to Year 10 pupils for carrying out an experiment to estimate the amount of energy available in peanuts and other foods and then to manage the class practical. After some discussion within the group, and with the recently covered work in the university fresh in their minds regarding the use of IT and investigations – the students proposed that the activity be presented as an investigation, the object being to develop the skills needed to carry out whole investigations which had been identified by the teacher as being a weak aspect of the pupils' work. After a brainstorming session where the 'prediction strand' would be addressed, the students suggested that a demonstration using a datalogging technique could be followed by the groups of pupils planning and carrying out their investigation with a view to analysing their results and drawing conclusions. Each student working with a group of four or five pupils was able to develop the pupils 'planning and doing' skills in terms of variables, fair testing and measurement precision. The approach was welcomed by the class teacher as an alternative to the one included in the scheme of work as it helped to address skills which would be needed later and presented the task in a way that did not merely require pupils to 'follow a recipe'. Maynard and Furlong (1993, p.72) identify one of the stages of development in trainee teachers as 'hitting the plateau' where once an approach is found that seems to work it is usually adhered to. Teachers participating in the exercise indicated that other pressures on their time tended to restrict the styles and strategies used to capture the attention of pupils and motivate them.

> It was very useful having the four students. Although teachers should make lessons interesting the shortage of time often prevents this happening; there is a tendency to be less creative in the normal course of events and having four different suggestions for organising and presenting information gets you to acknowledge other approaches at the very least... it takes you out of the routine approach. The use of datalogging to do the initial demonstration on comparing the energy available from different foods is one that I have now used with another class. (Teacher C)

In the second example, another group of students was asked to cover the preparation, collection and testing of gases. The 'normal' approach was for pupils to be shown the preparation and collection of three different gases and to follow this up by testing each gas with the appropriate test using a worksheet. Again, in discussion that ensued within the group of students, and with the teacher-tutor and the university tutor, a different approach was proposed to take advantage of the number of adults in the room and the fact that this was the third encounter with the class and the students were beginning to appreciate the strengths and needs of the four or five pupils in their group. A more interactive and, to some extent differentiated, approach was made possible. Pupils were given a collection of cut-out diagrams illustrating the types of apparatus set-ups used in the preparation and collection of gases followed by a simple table with data of the properties of some gases. They were then asked to select the most suitable apparatus set-up for some of the gases in the table and then to justify their decision. The range and complexity of the examples used were governed by the students' knowledge of the individuals in their group. A classic illustration for all that differentiation in action is possible if it can be made more manageable, and that a better pupil-teacher ratio is one requirement, albeit not on the scale used here! The comments of the teacher sums up the benefits derived in this instance but could be applied equally to others.

> The different strategy that the students decided to use certainly got the pupils involved and they appeared to understand it; it certainly seemed more logical and what is more they remembered it much later. The strategy and the resource have now been included in the department resource file for possible future use. (Teacher D)

Where teachers 'led the lesson' the requirement to produce a brief lesson plan with objectives and 'signposting' of possible critical events/incidents/behaviour for students to observe and later discuss was in itself seen to have a positive effect in the teachers' own work.

> The lessons tended to be given more thought and resulted in me being in greater control of the lesson. The advantages of lesson planning was brought to the fore again; you know that it is a good idea. (Teacher B)

> I needed to have clear thoughts in order to inform the students and it made me think of the aims and objectives for lessons. (Teacher D)

> I didn't find the idea of 'signposting' easy. My own skills of identifying and observing critical situations have been sharpened and helped me analyse lessons more critically. (Teacher D)

Further advantages were seen by the teachers to extend into other areas of their work in preparation for what they will be expected to do for appraisal and OFSTED inspections. In fact the exercise focusing on the learning objectives has contributed to the deliberations of the assessment working group in the school.

The presence of the students also acted as a spur to use approaches with groups that might have not been used in normal circumstances. One teacher who had previously only used a database on the network with more able and competent pupils because it was deemed to be excessively problematic to be used with less competent pupils, was able to successfully use the network with this group where the students acted as troubleshooters. The debrief that followed was extremely useful to all concerned as it addressed equal opportunity issues which fed into later parts of the programme both in the school and at the university.

The advantages of having the students in lessons were not only seen in terms of the direct benefit to pupils but also how teachers saw their charges. In a class, described as having 'special needs' groups, where the teacher felt unable to deal with 'all the needs of the pupils' and found that in the normal course of a lesson some pupils' needs were often ignored, the presence of several students in lessons helped to alleviate the problem.

> They got work out of all the pupils, who enjoyed the attention they received. The pupils were excited about the prospect of having other adults working with them and felt treated in a special way; they looked forward to having their student. (Teacher C – in her second year of teaching)

The extra supervision, which enabled more pupils to contribute in the lesson, gain rapid positive feedback, and seek immediate help with areas that posed problems, meant that interest and motivation were maintained for longer than was normally the case and altered the perceptions held by teachers.

> The close attention pupils received, with students as team leaders, enabled pupils to be kept on task – the pupils enjoyed it and it made me see that they were capable of more than I had anticipated, having previously categorised them as unmotivated and lacking ability. (Teacher B)

Continuous demands on the teacher during lessons often means that the opportunity to stand back and take a look at how pupils work is very limited and the presence of the student teachers enabled this to be done while the pupils still carry on with their normal coursework.

> It made me realise that Darren's problem was that he could not concentrate rather than being just lazy. My relationship with him is different now; I don't have to go at him but try and provide him with constant reminders. (Teacher C)

> It was very useful watching pupils interacting with the students as it helped me to realise further their problems in communicating; as a result I was able to give particular pupils more time. (Teacher A)

While the advantages of having the four student teachers in the lesson was readily acknowledged there was some additional work and advanced organisation needed on the part of the teachers. Any thoughts that this would be proved to be unacceptable were unfounded.

> It is not a drain on teachers' time as it was organised to fit in with existing plans. Any disadvantages were outweighed by the advantages. (Teacher C)

> Onerous in terms of time – yes, may be; but to talk to students about work you need to put some planning into it. The benefits outweighed the extra work. (Teacher B)

The volume of work for the technicians must not be underestimated and their co-operation and enthusiasm for the partnership arrangements are just as important as those of the teachers involved; without them most of the ideas of the students and teachers would have remained just that!

The slight anxiety expressed at the outset was seen to be more than compensated for by the 'feel good' factor that resulted and the students' eagerness and enthusiasm were seen to outweigh their lack of experience. While the gains for the staff and pupils might not be earth shattering to some, they were considered to be sufficiently significant for the participants to express an interest in being involved the following year.

An INSET potential that is actually cheap and one that could be developed further by building on this year's experience. (Teacher B)

Epilogue

There were clearly positive outcomes from the serial school-based experience for the pupils, teachers and students. The realisation of the professional development potential of involvement with initial teacher training was important. Students' experiences were gained at first hand and the exercise permitted them to construct and test out some elements of their own theories of class management, group work and questioning skills.

The early days in the training of teachers need not be all 'give and no take' on the part of schools and 'all take and no give' on the part of students and the HEI; rather it is hoped that the account above clearly illustrates that all parties in the partnership are able to 'give and take' to the mutual benefit of all concerned and will encourage schools and departments to consider working with HEIs in all phases of ITT.

Appendix

The University of Birmingham
School of Education

PGCE Main Method Religious Education

Checklist for Evaluation of Initial Teaching Skills

(A) The use of the chalkboard and overhead projector
Using the chalkboard
1. Position of the chalkboard? Can it be seen by all pupils?
2. Is the board clean before lesson begins? If not, does the student clean it before commencing to teach?
3. Are chalks and duster available before the lesson?
4. Is the writing large enough?
5. Is the writing too faint?
6. Is the writing level?
7. Is the writing in a uniform style (i.e. no mixtures of upper and lower case letters)? Are capital letters avoided?
8. Are punctuation marks clearly defined?
9. Are spellings corrected?
10. Does the student avoid 'talking to the board'?
11. For what purpose is the board used (e.g. incidentally for spellings and new words; as an aid to explanation)? Is there a clearly defined area of the chalkboard for such incidental use?
12. Is the board used as a means of emphasising points during the lesson? Are different coloured chalks used?
13. Is the board used to present summaries of main points?
14. Is the summary built up during the course of the lesson?
15. Does the summary follow a logical sequence?
16. If pupils are required to copy from the board, is a check kept on their progress before work is wiped off?
17. Does the student prepare the board with work *before* the lesson?

The use of the overhead projector

1. Does the student check that the OHP is working before commencing the lesson?
2. Does the student check that the pens are working before commencing the lesson? Are they permanent or washable?
3. Is the screen properly angled and visible to all pupils?
4. Does the OHP have a continuous acetate roll? Is it torn?
5. Has the student prepared transparencies before the lesson?
6. Are the transparencies framed? Do they make use of layering?
7. Does the student avoid 'turning and talking to the screen'?
8. Does the student avoid exposing writing which is to follow?
9. Does the student switch off when the visual display is no longer needed or is the OHP left running regardless?
10. Does the student fully exploit the advantages of using an OHP?
11. Check items relevant from those given for using chalkboards.

(B) Use of voice/speech

1. Does the student modulate his/her voice?
2. Can he/she be heard at the back of the classroom without shouting?
3. Does he/she speak too quickly/too slowly?
4. Does he/she use the voice for dramatic effect? How?
5. Does he/she avoid long, complex sentences?
6. Does he/she avoid verbal mannerisms?
7. Does he/she avoid non-verbal mannerisms?
8. Does he/she *communicate* effectively with the class?
9. Is his/her voice interesting to listen to?
10. Is slang avoided?
11. Is his/her accent a barrier to communication?
12. Does he/she talk too much? Does the student listen to the children?
13. Does the student have 'lightness of touch' or is he/she 'heavy handed'? Does he/she use humour?
14. Does he/she make good eye contact with individuals and the class when he/she is talking to them?
15. Does he/she make appropriate use of gesture to reinforce verbal communication?
16. Does the student give instructions clearly? Are they written on the board?
17. Is the student boring?

(C) Exposition of content

1. Does the student show interest and enthusiasm?
2. Is the material appropriately sequenced?

3. Are the main points emphasised? How?
4. Is the student's vocabulary and sentence structure suitable?
5. Does he/she write technical terms on the board and explain them?
6. Does the student make periodic checks to ensure that pupils are following his/her explanations? How?
7. Does the student succeed in arousing pupils' interests?
8. Is the content appropriate to the pupils' development levels?
9. Does the student provide a sufficient number of interesting examples which illustrate a concept or a principle?
10. Does the student present the content by means of more than one modality (e.g. visually as well as verbally)?

(D) Techniques of questioning
1. Are 'Yes' or 'No' questions avoided? Are 'chorus' answers avoided?
2. Does the student use a question instead of telling pupils something?
3. Are the questions well-phrased and clearly expressed?
4. Are questions used as a means of class control?
5. Are questions used to introduce the lesson?
6. Are questions used to revise a lesson?
7. Does the student ask too many questions?
8. Does the student 'cue' responses from the pupil?
9. Does the student address questions to individuals by name?
10. Does the student insist on 'Hands up' before answering?
11. Does the student avoid asking the first pupil with his/her hand up?
12. Does the student recognise when it is time to give an answer him/herself?
13. Does the student repeat a pupil's answer so that everyone can benefit from it?
14. Is the student encouraging, even when the answers are wrong?
15. Does the student respond to *all* answers? Does he/she use sufficient praise to ensure positive responses in the future?
16. Does the student avoid sarcasm?
17. Can the student think up questions quickly or is he/she dependent upon asking prepared questions?
18. Are written questions previously prepared and well-phrased?

(E) Preparation and use of Visual Aids
1. Is the aid simple, emphasising teaching points that the student wishes to make?
2. Is the aid appropriate – in size, in content, in application?

3. How is the aid presented? How is it displayed?
4. Does the student avoid 'hiding behind' or 'talking to' the aid?
5. Are labels readable, bold, neatly written?
6. Does the student avoid passing small pictures around the class?

(F) Organisation of a classroom activity

1. Does the student give adequate explanations about what the pupils are to do? Are the instructions clear? Does he/she check that everyone has understood what is expected of them?
2. Are the seating arrangements appropriate? Might seating have been arranged before the lesson? How was seating arranged during the lesson?
3. Are all the materials readily available? How were these distributed?
4. Does the student move quickly round the class to get all pupils started?
5. Is the student 'aware' of what is happening in the classroom at all times?
6. Is help given to individuals when necessary?
7. How does the student keep a check on the progress of different groups?
8. Does the student insist on adequate standards in relation to pupils' work or does he/she accept anything?
9. How is the activity brought to a conclusion? Is the lesson concluded just *before* the bell with everything packed away neatly?
10. How does the student intend to evaluate the success or otherwise of the lesson?

(G) Techniques of class control

1. Is the student in the classroom before the pupils?
2. Does the student establish order in the corridor *before* the pupils enter the classroom?
3. Does the student make his/her presence obvious as the pupils enter? How?
4. Does the student settle the class quickly in their seats?
5. Does the student establish quiet and attention before starting the lesson?
6. Does the student check that all pupils are present and so gauge the right moment to start the lesson without fear of latecomers interrupting the start?
7. Does the student start the lesson in an interesting manner? How?

8. Does the student get the pupils involved in an activity early in the lesson?
9. Does the student have a procedure for distributing materials?
10. Does the student have spare pens and pencils?
11. Does the student have something prepared for those pupils who 'finish first'? Are tasks and teaching materials differentiated?
12. Does the student avoid talking/shouting above noise?
13. Is the student aware of potentially disruptive pupils?
14. Are any difficulties a consequence of the seating arrangements?
15. Does the student take every opportunity to give praise and so positively reinforce good behaviour?
16. Is the student vigilant? Does he/she give the impression of being aware of everything and everyone?
17. Does the student avoid threats which cannot be carried through?
18. Does the student avoid confrontations and look for ways of distracting students from evil intent?
19. Does the student make use of pupils' names?
20. Is the student's manner pleasant but firm?
21. Does the student have a procedure for dismissing the class at the end of the lesson?
22. Is the student interesting and confident?

(H) Methods of assessment (marking)
1. Is the student aware of the school's system of marking and record-keeping?
2. Does the student keep up to date with marking?
3. Does the student seek opportunities to write encouraging remarks on pupils' work?
4. Does the student inform the pupils of his/her marking procedure? Does he/she explain what is 'good' work?
5. Does the student take an opportunity to discuss the pupils' work? Is this done individually, or as a class?
6. Does the student seek an opportunity to display pupils' work?
7. Does the student keep personal records as well as marks?
8. Does the student spend too much/too little time on going over homework?

References

Bailey, P. (1974) *Teaching Geography*. London: David and Charles.

Barber, M. (1993) 'The Truth about Partnership', *Journal of Education for Teaching*, **19**(3), pp.255–262.

Barber, M. (1994) 'Born to be better', *Times Educational Supplement*, 18 March.

Beardon, T., Booth, M., Hargreaves, D. and Reiss, M. (1992) *School-led initial teacher training – the way forward*. Cambridge: Cambridge University, Department of Education.

Bell, S., Brown, P. and Buckley, S. (1992) *Hole Numbers*. London: Cambridge University Press.

Bennett, C., Jones, B. and Maude, P. (1994) 'Insights from the Teaching Profession: potential advantages and disadvantages of greater school involvement in ITE', *Cambridge Journal of Education*, **24**(1), pp.67–73.

Berrill, M. (1994) 'ITE Crossroads or By-pass?', *Cambridge Journal of Education*, **24**(1), pp.113–115.

Bines, H. (1992) 'Quality or survival? The consultation document on the reform of initial teacher training for secondary education', *Journal of Education Policy,* **7**(5), pp.511–519.

Bolton, E. (1994) 'One last push', *Guardian Education*, 17 May.

Brunsden, D. (1987) 'The Science of the Unknown', *Geography,* **72**(2), pp.193–208.

Butt, G. (1994) 'Assessment through residential fieldstudy in the Geography PGCE', in S. Butterfield (Ed.) *Qualifying Teachers: assessing professional work*. (Educational Review Publications, No. 2.)

Butterworth, M. (1989) 'Student reactions to videotape feedback of teaching performance', *Bulletin of Physical Education*, **25**(3), pp.37–41.

CATE (1992) *The Accreditation of Initial Teacher Training Under Circulars 9/92 (Department for Education) and 35/92 (Welsh Office). A note of guidance from the Council for the Accreditation of Teacher Education*. London: Council for the Accreditation of Teacher

Education.

Clarke, K. (1992) Speech presented to North of England Education Conference, 4 January.

Cohen, L. and Manion, L. (1989) *Research Methods in Education* (Third Edition). London: Routledge.

Cooper, C. and Latham, J. (1988) 'Visits Out of School', *Teaching Geography*, **13**(2), pp.72–3.

DES (1989) *Safety in Outdoor Education*. London: HMSO.

DES (1990) *English in the National Curriculum*. London: HMSO.

DES (1991a) *Geography in the National Curriculum*. London: HMSO.

DES (1991b) *History in the National Curriculum*. London: HMSO.

DES/HMI (1991) *School-based Initial Teacher Training in England and Wales*. London: HMSO.

DfE (1992) *Initial Teacher Training (Secondary Phase): Circular 9/92*. London: DfE.

DfE (1993) *The Government's Proposals for the Reform of Initial Teacher Training*. London: DfE.

Dunne, M., Lock, R. and Soares, A. (forthcoming) Partnership in Initial Teacher Training: After the Shotgun Wedding.

Edwards, T. (1994) 'Universities Council for Education of Teachers: defending an interest or fighting a cause?', *Journal of Education for Teaching*, **20**(2), pp.143–152.

Frost, D. (1993) 'Mentoring and the New Partnership', in D. McIntyre, H. Hagger, and M. Wilkin (Eds) *Mentoring: Perspectives on School-based Teacher Education*. London: Kogan Page.

Geographical Association (1984) Sixth Form – University Working Group, 'The enduring purpose of fieldwork', *Teaching Geography*, **9**(5), pp.209–211.

Griffiths, M. and Tann, S. (1992) 'Using reflective practice to link personal and public theories', *Journal of Education for Teaching*, **18**(1).

Haigh, G. (1994) 'A Reflection on Good Practice', *Times Educational Supplement,* 10 June.

Hall, D. (1976) *Geography and the Geography Teacher*. London: Allen and Unwin.

Hargreaves, D. (1990) *The Future of Teacher Education*. London: Hockerill Educational Foundation.

Hart, C. and Thomas, T. (1986) 'Framework Fieldwork', in D. Boardman (Ed.) *Handbook for Geography Teachers*. Geographical Association.

Hawkins, E. (1988) (Ed.) *Intensive Language Teaching and Learning*. Centre for Information on Language Teaching and Research.

Hawkins, G. (1987) 'From awareness to participation; New directions in the outdoor experience', *Geography*, **72**(2), pp.217–221.

Hill, J.E. and Kerber, A. (1967) *Models, Methods and Analytical Procedures in Educational Research.* Detroit: Wayne State University Press.

Hopkins, D. (1993) *A Teacher's Guide to Classroom Research* (Second Edition). Milton Keynes: Open University Press.

Lawlor, S. (1990) *Teachers Mistaught – training in theories or education in subjects?* London: Centre for Policy Studies.

Lawlor, S. (1992) 'A Touch of Class for Teachers', *The Times*, 6 January.

Lidstone, J. (1988) 'Teaching and Learning Geography through Fieldwork', in R. Gerber and J. Lidstone, *Developing Skills in Geographical Education.* Brisbane: IGU/Jacaranda Press.

Maynard, T. and Furlong, J. (1993) 'Learning to Teach and Models of Mentoring', in D. McIntyre, H. Hagger and M. Wilkin (Eds) *Mentoring: Perspectives on School-based Teacher Education.* London: Kogan Page.

McIntyre, D., Hagger, H. and Wilkin, M. (1993) (Eds) *Mentoring: Perspectives on School-based Teacher Education.* London: Kogan Page.

McIntyre, D. and Hagger, H. (1993) 'Teachers' Expertise and Models of Mentoring', in D. McIntyre, H. Hagger and M. Wilkin (Eds) *Mentoring: Perspectives on School-based Teacher Education.* London: Kogan Page.

McPartland, M. and Harvey, P. (1987) 'A Question of Fieldwork', *Teaching Geography,* June.

NCC (1992) *Using and Applying Mathematics, Book A.* York: National Curriculum Council.

O'Hear, A. (1988) *Who Teaches the Teachers?* London: Social Affairs Unit.

OHMCI (1993) *The Articled Teacher Scheme. September 1990–July 1992.* London: HMSO.

Passey, D. and Ridgway, J. (1994) 'The Current Impact of IT, and the Stages of School IT Development: Are There Any Prospects for the Future?', *Computer Education,* February, pp.2–5.

Pearce, T. (1987) 'Teaching and Learning Through Direct Experience', in P. Bailey and T. Binns *A Case for Geography.* Sheffield: The Geographical Association.

Pocock, D. (1983) 'Geographical fieldwork: an experiential perspective', *Geography,* 68, pp.315–325.

Raw, M. (1989) 'Organising an A level Fieldcourse', in P. Wiegand (Ed.) *Managing the Geography Department.* Sheffield: The Geographical Association.

SCAA (1994) *Geography Draft Proposals.* London: HMSO.

SHA (1993) *Some Practical Advice, SHA Update No 28.* Secondary Heads Association.

Siedentop, D. (1983) *Developing Teaching Skills in Physical Education* (Second Edition). Palo Alto: Mayfield Publishing Co.

Smith, P. (1987) 'Outdoor Education and Its Educational Objectives', *Geography*, **72**(2), pp.209–216.

Stone, V. (1993) 'Where...? Establishing the framework for partnership – principles and practice', in J. Thoroughgood *Partners.* Centre for Information on Language Teaching and Research.

Tebbutt, M.J. (1993) 'IT in Science Education – A Clouded Vision?', *Australian Educational Computing*, 8, pp.239–244.

Thomas, T. (1990) *Geography Outside the Classroom.* Sheffield: The Geographical Association.

Watts, R. (1993) 'Why site visits?', *Welsh Historian*, 20, pp.15–18.

Wilkin, M. (1992) (Ed.) *Mentoring in Schools.* London: Kogan Page.

Wilkin, M. (1993) 'Initial Training as a Case of Post-modern Development: Some Implications for Mentoring', in D. McIntyre, H. Hagger and M. Wilkin (Eds) *Mentoring: Perspectives on School-based Teacher Education.* London: Kogan Page.

Williams, E.A. (1993) 'The Reflective Physical Education Teacher: Implications for Initial Teacher Education', *Physical Education Review*, **16**(2), pp.137–144.

Williams, E.A. (1994) 'Roles and Responsibilities in Initial Teacher Training – student views', *Educational Studies*, **20**(2), pp.167–180.

Wright, N. (1993) 'Counting the cost of students in classrooms', *Education*, 27 August, pp.156–157.

Index

Wright 4

Year 10 7, 32, 66, 101, 105, 107, 116
Year 11 101
Year 7 40, 41, 66, 86, 87, 98, 105
Year 8 13, 54, 66, 74, 86, 91, 98, 105, 106
Year 9 40, 54, 55, 66, 74, 98, 101